*For Renée,*

*who has asked all of these questions
at one time or another.*

# Contents

# Forward

*Holy Noise* is cleverly conceived, dragged from the fiery furnace of great experience. It is also brilliantly written. Who should read this book? Everyone who has an interest in worship and church music would benefit. It offers a window into that somewhat murky and mysterious thing that happens when churches gather.  Every church member could benefit, but for those who dedicate their gifts to worshipping God through music, it is a must.

I had the privilege to work with Dr. Ken Powers for almost a decade. We shared the leadership in a Presbyterian church; he led the music and I served as Pastor. He has now completed 14 years at this same church, which has to be some kind of record for service in a music program.

Ken has always paid attention to the complicated process of communication, the lack of which imperils the functioning of any organization. No one is better equipped to talk about the questions that come up in the course of directing music. He has a diversity of experience in church music serving different size churches. Added to his wealth of experience has been the opportunity to earn several advanced degrees.

While we were working together, I was always amazed how Ken was a non-anxious presence. "Grace under fire" is another way to say it. By asking more of a choir than they had to give, somehow they became more than they were. Ken is a maestro who steps into his role giving his best and asking for the same from those who surround him in service. The groups under his baton always reach beyond their ability, and in doing so arrive at new levels of confidence and competence. Many times I marveled through the years as musical gifts were offered to God in our congregation, and when they were over, Ken would quietly disappear, step back, and never allow himself to be idolized or even properly thanked for his hard work. For him, his work at church is a gift to God, not a performance.

I spent four years in Christian Spirituality at Columbia Seminary before my retirement. These years were times of reflection. I had always known that music goes where words can't travel. I solidified my belief that worship shapes us spiritually in ways that nothing else approaches. In his opus, Ken shares his gift for putting words around the music that makes devotional offerings to God. That's the real beauty of the pages you are holding in your hands. Here you discover and uncover a treasury of reflections on ordinary questions that call upon scripture and other spiritual writings for clarity. The Psalms teach us that song is prayer and prayer is song. And so the approach of reflection and prayerful offering of music exist as a whole different environment for the spiritual growth of believing people. In reading this book you will get a glimpse of Dr. Powers' "tongue in cheek," almost biting humor as well as his deliberately constructed responses to all the question of church musicians, which, inevitably lead to more questions and ultimately to the timeless mystery that is God.

Rev. Thomas G. Lewis, D.Min.
Retired Director of Spirituality Program
Columbia Theological Seminary

# Preface

I am a church musician, and, as one of my mentors used to say, I am in the listening business. Throughout my career, I have become skilled at the art of listening to church people at church. After all, it is my job to offer a discerning ear and to give feedback on what I hear in the music. I have learned to listen to more than the music. I have learned to listen to the questions that people make as they offer their talents. I hear them honing their skills for God. These questions have filled what would have been many of the silent spaces between episodes of music making, and, everywhere I have been, they have been the same. The Southern Baptist, United Methodist, and Presbyterian (U.S.A.) churches that I have served have had different ways of organizing and doing church, different people filling their pews, different architectural styles in which they assembled, and different methods of performing mission activities. However, the questions...the basic questions asked around and about the music and worship-related matters have been the same.

We have varying levels of giftedness that grow by training and persistent experiences. By the grace of God, we are better than the products of our experiences, although we carry images and words in our heads that render repeat performances more often than we would like. Our most serious questions come from these. We all have them. We all are creatures of worth. Our issues go forth, and our talents flourish or languish under life's sun and rain.

Looking back, I cannot believe that my minister of music gave me the opportunity, at a tender age, to direct a children's choir at our church. A few of the singers were only a couple of years my junior and hardly open, as I recall, to taking direction from one of their peers. The only musical qualifications I had were those I had gained in school. That was almost 40 years ago.

Except for brief episodes of transition, never lasting more than a few weeks or months, my life has never lost its intimate identification with music and God's people in pursuit of God's glory. I have found my life's work to be a response to a divine calling that I have cherished. There is no way for me to calculate the number of rehearsals nor the times of worship that I have led, attended, or encountered; nevertheless, the notion comes mightily upon me that I would be more than glad to do them all again. In the company of brother and sister believers I have found acceptance, nurture, challenge, and grace as we have labored together to offer sacrifices of praise and devotion that God desires and deserves.

I am not the same person that I was then. I have experienced triumphs. I have disappointed. I have sinned. I have known forgiveness –and yet, in important ways, I am just an older version of the boy who made his solo debut in Kindergarten. As I write this, I remember life events that shaped me, stretched and twisted my faith, but never broke my will. I recall moments of transcendence as I have witnessed God alive in others and in myself. Through the idea of the power of God at work in the world and in individual lives, coupled with the ineffable emotions wrought by the gift of music in expressing the wonder of service, my journey has found clarity and sustenance.

This book seeks to order some questions we bring about music to church and to make sense out of the "holy noise" that infiltrates our lives as music about our Lord *moves us to a more profound "Alleluia."*[1] The idea for this investigation started in my heart and mind years ago when I was on a spiritual retreat in the mountains. Now, much, much later, I

---

[1] from the hymn, *When in Our Music God Is Glorified*, F. Pratt Green, 1972, Hope Publishing Co.

have finally gotten around to writing it. A more comprehensive treatment of these important issues results because of the procrastination. This happened in God's time.

# Introduction

The readers of this book are those who identify with the ministry of music within their churches. Some will be the music ministers, directors, or those who go by similar titles. Others will be the ones who play the common, traditional instruments of the church, the organ and piano. Still others will be the ones who rehearse weekly in choirs and ensembles as singers and ringers. Another group will be the ones who play band and orchestra instruments in their churches. The person who does not fall into any of these categories has either picked up this book by mistake, thinking it was about something else, or one who truly wants to know the things that race through the minds of church music people as they do their work and fulfill their roles within congregational life. All are welcome to these pages.

People tell us from an early age to ask questions of a teacher when we do not understand something. Little children routinely ask their parents questions about how things work, what certain words mean, or if they can go over to a friend's house to play. We get the feeling, early on, that questions are important. It is only later in life, as we mature, that we begin to question our questions. If we ask this or that, people will think we are not intelligent. We want to ask a question, but we do not understand enough to know how to ask.

Gregory Stock's *The Book of Questions* (1987)[1] was unique in its form. Its inimitable appearance into the literary world challenged readers to change the ways in which they viewed the world. Without offering a single opinion of his own, Stock posed more than 250 questions. More recently, writers (Browne & Keeley, 2000),[2] and (Miller, 2004)[3] have touted personal accountability in work and in life and critical ways of thinking. Learning to question assists us in achieving the things that are important to us.

We grow when we question things. Questions can lead to the clarification of our musical offerings and our worship of God. Questioning helps us to achieve understanding. Fundamental to faith development is the question of *questions*. Thomas Merton observed that if we are to understand anything about the Bible, we must ask, "What kind of book is this" (Merton, 1970, p. 11)?[4] We learn when we inquire. In any group, it helps to know where we have been, where we are, and where we intend to go and grow. Questioning provides a continuous means by which these goals reach answers.

Seventeen types of questions appear herein, treating questions as tools for learning (McKenzie, 1997).[5] This taxonomy serves as the outline for the text. Question (English). Frage (German). Pregunta (Spanish). By whatever name, *questioning* plays itself out universally.

Both Old and New Testaments are replete with questions. Throughout this narrative, a few of Jesus' questions as recorded in the Gospels align with the categorical sections that find treatment here.

> God to Adam: "Have you eaten from the tree of which I commanded you not to eat?" (Genesis 3:11); God to Moses: "What is that in your right hand?" (Exodus 4:2); God to Paul: "Saul, Saul, why do you persecute me?" (Acts 9:4); God (the Son) to God (the Father): "Why have You forsaken Me"? (Matthew 27:46)

The best questions require measured responses from the ones they address. Some questions require the straightforward "yes" or "no." Some questions call for qualified responses that seek to define what the question is trying to call forth. There are questions that produce more questions. In addition, there are questions that are not questions at all, for the one asking them already knows the answer. Also, let us not forget the questions that defer answer to other times and places. Questioning suggests that there is a conversation at some level.

God still asks questions. The ones recorded in the Holy Bible are not the end of God's interrogation of humankind. The Holy Spirit dwells within believers' lives, stoking continual questions and igniting on-going dialogue between God and God's chief creation.

Great questions have haunted humanity throughout the ages. People have used their intellect and skill to ascertain answers from the natural world and the realm of heaven to unlock many of life's mysteries.

The function of questions needs a clear understanding. Within the context of church, believers should be on guard that questioning might reveal answers that congregations do not want to wrestle with or acknowledge. With questioning, comes the responsibility of searching for truth. The Good News is that, through Jesus Christ, the truth will set us free. I hold a personal view of questions. I am wary of one who seems to have life all figured out. I tend to ignore those who claim to have all answers for all problems.

This book takes its form around a fact of church life. Churches use music to communicate to God in worship. Churches have musical groups that rehearse in preparation for worship. Music just does not happen on its own. Wherever there are church musicians, there are questions. Some of them are hilarious. Some church questions surface from time to time and repeat. There are those that no one tries to answer, so the questioner keeps asking the same questions instead of trying to figure out why no one is answering.

I remember, as a preschooler, wondering what was going on as I sat on the ground under a tent one summer in my hometown, watching an evangelist sweat his way across the platform and my fascination with the immense canopy that served as a roof for that outdoor tabernacle. I do not remember the sermon or the music, but I vividly remember the songbook that I used to push around the wood shavings that blanketed the floor. I had questions.

I remember the feelings that I had with my touring youth choir while singing an evangelistic concert. I wondered if I had a call to Christian service. If I did, how was I going to know? I waited for voices to speak and the clouds to spell out my name. I needed to know how my gifts fit in to God's plan for my life. My feelings grabbed validation at several levels. Yet, I had more questions.

I remember walking in one of my graduation processions as the mighty pipe organ rose to greet my class. The power of the sound and the august nature of the occasion gave me the feeling that the will of God was upon me. I was about to launch my professional career. Was I not supposed to have most of the answers figured out? To my surprise, I knew I still had questions.

I remember chanting with Trappist Monks, retreating with them and trying, for a week, to share their unique lifestyle of work and prayer. We planted trees. We prayed. We tended the nursery. We prayed. We studied. We prayed. They are experts at listening. Their ministry is that of devotion. They inspired me to dig deeper so that I might go higher. They sang night and day. I had the answers that produced more questions.

I remember the trip to Asia, where I returned with a beautiful baby daughter, adopted from that mystic, ancient region. It was important to me to dedicate her to God in one of her home country's places of worship, even though that house was of a different faith. I remember another kind of chant as I stood in an incense-filled, Buddhist temple, praising Jesus for lots of answers and taking more questions to Him.

I remember standing over the hospital bed of my mother on her last day of life, singing songs of faith to her. I sang the ones that she loved the most. Even after she lacked the ability to speak to me, she heard the sounds of the hymns she learned as a girl in *the greatest generation,* a term coined by journalist Tom Brokaw to describe the generation of Americans who grew up during the Great Depression and then went on to fight in World War II.

She heard the songs that she had sung to me when I was too young to sing them for myself. She passed away with an unfurrowed brow. Carried away by the music of her cherished faith, she left this world without any questions. Thanks Be to God!

Of course, this one book does not pretend to ask or answer all of the questions that swirl around music at church –not even most of them, but it does cover of the most frequent ones that I have dealt with, and it helps church participants in constructing personal philosophies for Christian service. This book makes a *Holy Noise* – the kind that all faithful, spirit-led followers of Jesus Christ need to self-filter and refine as they live and serve.

Because of God's grace, extended for all, those of us who have placed our faith and trust in Him have songs worth sounding and questions that need airing as they flow through the sieve of our hearts and minds.

Kenneth E. Powers
October 2011

# I. Essential Questions

*Church musicians do more than make music. They ask questions that touch the heart and soul. Some of their questions are central to our lives as we search for meaning. Such questions are indispensable.*

*Jesus asked Essential Questions:*

- *How can anything good come out of an evil heart? (Matthew)*
- *Who do people say that I am? (Mark)*
- *Where is your faith? (Luke)*
- *Have I not chosen you? (John)*

# 1. May We Pray About That?

*Then, harmony reminds of a thing perfected. When we ponder the
perfect, we dream. When we dream, our thoughts inescapably turn
to heaven, our eternal home.*

Solomon once stood before an altar, erected in the court of
his people, and demonstrated to them his ability to be, not
only their King, but also their example. He chose to pray.

*Have regard to your servant's prayer and his plea, O Lord my
God, heeding the cry and the prayer that your servant prays to you
today.*
*~1 Kings 8:28*

The number of the Church's choir people who pray together
is legion. Prayer is a natural response to the nature of their
work. "But I come to choir to practice music. I do not want
choir turned into a prayer meeting. If I wanted to go to a
prayer group, I would join one," the disgruntled might say.
How are singers of songs and players of instruments
supposed to perform their duties together at church? Should
they keep things at an all business level, meaning that they
should stick to musical concerns only? Should they keep
their minds so fixed on the product of their efforts that they
neglect the processes that produce them?

The answers are *no* and *no*. Church music is a product-
oriented amalgamation of sacrifice offered to God during
formal times of devotion. It is one of the fruits of the
thankful. In addition, the process allows communities of
believers to communicate life's mountains and valleys.
Sopranos, altos, tenors, basses, keyboardists,
instrumentalists, and every other music group of the church
should feel the right and privilege of voicing, not only their
instrument, but themselves whenever they are surrounded

by others who have been born again by the regenerative power of the Spirit of the Lord God.

The songs we sing and play at church, in their own right, should be devotional. At any given time their texts, elevated by their tunes, rhythms, and harmonies, can speak as medicinal healing applied to our souls. Moreover, when we need to, we should stop the music and go to the prayers to which the music has sent us. It will help the music, shore up the places where we are weak, and commemorate the events that cause us to rejoice.

*Stand by us when we are speaking and when we hearing. In the name of the Intercessor we pray,* AMEN.

# 2. Is It All About You?

*When you perform, and the music is turning out the way you hoped and planned, it lives on its own. Even though you are the performer, it is almost as if you are an observer to its development. You are a part of the universe where you have latched on to the music, and it is taking you to a wonderful place.*

When we neglect our duty to God, we do not prosper. When we focus on ourselves, we rob ourselves of the blessings that come from providing service for others.

*You have sown much, and harvested little; you eat, but you never have enough; you drink, but you never have your fill; you clothe yourselves, but no one is warm; and you that earn wages earn wages to put them into a bag with holes.*
*~Haggai 1:6*

Dear Choir Member (*with apologies for the sarcasm*):

We are truly sorry for the way we have been treating you. We have been treating you like everyone else. We now realize that you are the most important one of us all and that without you and your numerous talents we would not be able to fulfill all of the responsibilities of our choir.

The truth is you are way beyond the rest of us in spiritual depth and maturity. We do well to look to you to emulate your words, actions, and practices. Pardon us for forgetting that everything we do should be in keeping with your needs, wants, and comforts.

You inspire us with your condescending attitude, your *better-than-thou* countenance, and your *don't you wish you had my taste in clothes* demeanor. What did we do before you joined the choir?

Several choir people have asked the director if you think our actions are merely extensions of your interpretations of Christian correctness and musical grace. We all think you do. We have learned that yielding to your guiding principles is the best and the only way to get along with you.

We are sorry that we cannot feel close to you. Maybe it is because you will not let us. Oh, well. Anyway, we are not worthy to approach you in a relaxed manner. We need to be on guard. It would just make you want to hurt our feelings.

Now we hear you are thinking of leaving our church. This makes us so very sad!

Sincerely,...*NOT!*

Your church choir friends

*Tell us again that everything is about You, and that nothing is about us. In the name of the Ancient of Days, AMEN.*

# 3. What is the Message of the Song?

*Music provides for us a path. The poet helps us to navigate that path in order to share the message of a song to everyone who would hear it.*

Our music causes us the attempt of singing or playing as one. We work together, bringing our numerous selves to a singular presence in worship. We present a singular message, showing our unity of spirit and God's unity of heart.

*Let anyone who has an ear listen.*
*~Revelation 9:13*

At church, it really does not matter how spine tingling the choral selection is—if it has nothing to say, then we should not be doing it there. The meaning here is obvious. Publishing a thing does not make it have a message that you and your church memberships agree with or endorse. When you sing, hear the words you are communicating. If you do not agree with them, then they will not minister as you would wish. If they say nothing to you, what can they possibly say to those who will hear?

Do not be confused by the style of music that wants to carry that message. You may not care for the kind of music you hear, but its message may be one that points people to the face of God. Conversely, you may love your Bluegrass Gospel song. Its chords may be soothing to your spirit, but its message may fall short of what you and your listeners truly believe about heaven.

We respect people who say what they mean and mean what they say. We respect them even when their interpretations of issues are different from our own. "Well, I'll say this for him," you will murmur, "You know where he stands." Let us be persistent in our attempts to procure, prepare, and present music that affirms what we know to be true and challenges what we want to improve to the glory of God, whose message in Christ Jesus reconciled Him to all who believe.

*Speak to us that we may hear. In the name of the Lord of Lords we pray,* AMEN.

# 4. Does He Have Friends?

*In the real world, people will hurt you with words and actions that sting. Things will harm you too. A great truth about music is that, while it will not always help you, it never will injure you.*

As priest and prophet, Zechariah wrote at times as a conversationalist- at other times as a poet. Here he talks about how the pretensions of a prophet caused suffering.

*And if anyone asks them, 'What are these wounds on your chest?' The answer will be 'The wounds I received in the house of my friends.' ~Zechariah 13:6*

I am shy.
I sing...
Not too loudly, but I sing.
I am with people who find it
Easy to express
The way they feel.
I make friends with the music.
That is where my comfort is.

I am alone.
I mingle...
Not too often, but I mingle.
I see church people who find it
Easy to say
"Let's do this," "See you tomorrow."
I make friends with the group
But not with individuals within it.

I am empty.
I live...
Not too often, but I live.
I work today and then go home,

Easy to do,
And to do all again tomorrow.
I make friends with routine.
Maybe someday I can join in life as God intends.

*Wrap your loving arms around us. In the name of the*
*Son of Man we pray, AMEN.*

# 5. Does That Sound Good?

*What does music mean? The answers to this question are as
numerous as there are hearers on the planet.*

A place inside of everyone hides from public view.
Christians should decorate that place.

*Rather, let your adornment be the inner self with the lasting
beauty of a gentle and quiet spirit, which is very precious in God's
sight.*
*~1 Peter 3:4*

Church musicians want their music to sound good. They
take pride in what they do. You will never hear a church
musician say, "I don't care how our music will sound. I want
to do a bad job for the Lord through the music of my
church." Round about are church choir people who will not
come to church on days when music that they do not think
sounds just right for worship is scheduled. They do not wish
for their names to be associated with something that does
not meet their high standards.

Often, as a way of checking and balancing, choir
members will suggest that a designated listener place
himself/herself at a distance from the choir during rehearsal
to listen for places that need correction. Just as solving the
problems of life are easier when they address issues from a
distance, so is correcting the quality of musical efforts more
effective when space exists between its origin and its impact.

We want our lives to sound good. When we suffer from
ill will with others or when relationships are strained or
when reputations take on injury through actions justly
reported or maliciously invented, we hurt, as do all who are
involved in the subterfuges of them all. Not only do church
musicians have to be concerned with the way their music
sounds, they have to be on guard that their lives match the

messages they proclaim. It is possible that those messages could be off key as well as off target. God is available, not from a distance, but from within. God molds, mends, and loves those who love Him and follow His purposes.

*Sound forth the reconciling music of Your Spirit Holy. In the name of Yahweh we pray, AMEN.*

# 6. Does Time Mean Anything?

*Music is like freezing time in a way and inspecting it quite closely in interesting ways.*

It is one thing to be quiet. It is another thing to be silent. Christians need to know when to wait patiently for God's time.

*Therefore, the prudent will keep silent in such a time;*
*for it is an evil time.*
*~Amos 5:13*

Tardy. Unusually early. Punctual. Fashionably late. We describe the ways we manage time, often using words like these. We say "our time," for the time is ours. Time exists for us in equal measure by the one, true God who gives us our days. It does not matter where you live or in which socioeconomic strata you are situated, each of us holds the same amount of time. A 24-hour day is the same the world over, regardless of the amount of sunshine, darkness, rain, snow, or driving wind that gives witness in it. We focus on things important to us when we write down what we want, find out what time means, identify our values, and create visions.[6] Church music people are rehearsing people. It is wise for leaders to start when they have agreed to start and end when they have agreed to end, regardless of attendance or timeliness of the participants. Church people hold services of worship to bring honor and glory to the Lord Jesus. These services need to begin when they are supposed to begin. They need to end...when they need to end.

You are in a music rehearsal. You waste three minutes of time. There are 20 people there. You have wasted, not three minutes, but 60 minutes of collective time. Time is synonymous with life. We do not wish to waste our lives; neither do we want to waste our time.

Music reminds us of this on its every visitation, for it is constructed in units that are organized in time. These time signatures tell performers how to count the seconds that will turn into minutes as the music blossoms as a flower.

Time. Spend it for God. Spend time making music for God. God's time and God's music are eternal.

*Count on us to count on You. In the name of the Rose of Sharon we pray,* AMEN.

# II. Organizing Questions

*Church musicians come with varying degrees of organizational gifts. Their questions relative to associations make it possible to structure their findings into categories that allow them to construct meaning.*

<u>*Jesus asked Organizing Questions:*</u>

- *Who is my mother? Who are my brothers? (Matthew)*
- *With what comparison shall we liken the Kingdom of God? (Mark)*
- *Who is greater, the guest or the servant? (Luke)*
- *You do not believe earthly things, so do you believe heavenly things? (John)*

# 7.  Can We Have a Band?

*Some instruments we love. Some instruments we loathe. Some instruments we can take or leave.*

The Levitical leaders trained the Israelites as singers and instrumentalists for solemn processions.

*David also commanded the chiefs of the Levites to appoint their kindred as the singers to play on musical instruments, on harps and lyres and cymbals, to raise loud sounds of joy.*
*~1 Chronicles 15:16*

The bread and butter choir of the church is the congregation. There can be no substitute choir for the people of God, as a whole, offering praise together in song. The most common chord at church is struck by those who sing, and many larger churches are able to augment their standard singing choirs with instrumental ensembles, and even orchestras, to provide choice in musical praise to those thusly talented.

Church music leaders minister when they take the time to poll members about instruments. One has a saxophone stowed away in a dusty attic. Another has a cello that has been silent since high school. Many people who once played in bands or orchestras do not play at present because they have no place to play. There are those, of course, who have maintained precise embouchures and bowing techniques by continuing to play in adulthood. We should not forget those in our churches who are still in school or college performing ensembles who are usually more than ready, willing, and able to bring their instruments to church and to accompany hymns and play service pieces.

The point of the question of church instruments is a valid one. We are not alike, although we train in the same musical ways. Each instrument sings in its own way, and when played by believers during times of prayer and praise, the songs are wondrously anointed.

So maybe you are in a church with an abundance of instrumentalists...professionals even. On the other hand, maybe you are like most congregations, and can round up a couple of trumpet players, a percussionist, and a violinist if you wanted to, or if you absolutely had to do so. Listen...I hear band people.

*Have mercy on us. In the name of the Horn of Salvation we pray,*
AMEN.

# 8. Do We Have to Wear Robes?

*It is droll. We learn music so that we can perform it. Then, we learn that we have also learned something about ourselves in the process. Usually, the harder the challenge presented by the music, the more the gain.*

Jesus asked His listeners if they found there a reed swaying in the breeze or a prophet, when they went to the desert to hear John the Baptist preach.

*What then did you go out to see? Someone dressed in soft robes? Look, those who put on fine clothing and live in luxury are in royal palaces.*
*~Luke 7:25*

You do not have to wear a choir robe to be a good praise-giver. [With no malice to people who are the choir robe business] A choir robe does not make you sound better; a strong case stands, however, that a robe makes you look better. A choir robe serves three undeniable functions:

1. A choir robe clothes each singer in a uniform manner. Military personnel match when they march. Sports teams unite under uniform colors and logos. Robes optically minimize diversities of body type and height. Choir people, who come in petite to plus sizes, become more cohesive, as if by magic, when they dress in common.
2. A choir robe furnishes each singer with immediate identification. When you are at church, and you see a robed figure, you know automatically that the person has some official function within the worship. Get real here. Have you ever seen a person put on a robe only to go sit on the back row? The robe says *this* person has prepared for worship.

3. A choir robe offers camouflage for that which can be distracting. If you get a new Easter dress, a new necktie, or a fabulous complete outfit at a bargain, you can be a choir person and still wear it to church. You just wear your robe on top of it during the service. O.K. Keep it real. If you and the rest of the choir figure prominently before the assembled body of believers, you do not want your couture to risk upstaging your message, now do you.

*Adorn us in righteousness. In the name of the Bridegroom we pray,* AMEN.

# 9. Is the Music in Error?

*Some people are born with a gift for interpreting music, for composing it, or for making sense of it. Some things come from above and cannot blossom from a classroom, a book, or in the laboratory of experience.*

In the waning paragraphs of the Old Testament, Malachi cries out to the Jews that there will be no shortage of people to magnify the name of the one, true God.

*For from the rising of the sun to its setting my name is great among the nations, and in every place incense is offered to my name, and a pure offering; for my name is great among the nations, says the LORD of hosts.*
*~Malachi 1:11*

"That chord at measure 50 does not sound just right," the conductor said. "Let's do it again. Let's start with the pick-up to that measure." The choir sings. "Hmm, I guess that was right after all," the conductor concluded with a shake of her head, adding, "There are times when the composer did not intend for it to be pretty. If we are to be faithful interpreters of the composer's ideas, we must sing what we see, even if it does not sound right to our disciplined ears."

"I was wondering the same thing," said the accompanist. That measure is weird for my part too. It sounds like a jumbled moment, and then it's gone."

"Well, one thing is for sure," the conductor said as she smiled. "If it sounds lovely right there, we are not doing it right." The singers laugh it off, but they do not feel confident. They long to sing those ugly chords again until the strange sounds solidify in their ears.

Then the truth starts to dawn on them. Elsie, in her quiet way, raises her hand with a gesture that would become her defining moment, retold down through the years in that church's choir lore. "I believe that there is a misprint. I think that the A in the soprano part in measure 50 should be an A flat on the third beat and the beat four B in the tenor part should be flat also."

The singers sit in stunned hushes. Complete silence. Crickets chirp outside.

Then a round of applause ensues for the one who dared to challenge the printed page.

*In the name of the Master we pray,* AMEN.

# 10. Where is Your Pencil?

*It is sobering. Your love for music will never make you a household name or cause you to become rich. Then you realize that it gives you something you can claim for yourself.*

Even in times of misery, Jude's New Testament voice fills the air with the news that God's love multiplies through acts of tranquility and forgiveness.

*May, mercy, peace, and love be yours in abundance.*
*~Jude 1:2*

"The shortest pencil is longer than the longest memory," the music minister said during a tedious moment in the rehearsal. "We have stopped to fix that spot more times than I care to remember. Stop making the same mistake...mark your music...please." A few of the singers and instrumentalists took out their pencils and marked the music as their leader requested. A few of the others would have gladly done that, but they did not have a pencil. Still more, assured of their ability to remember, did not move a muscle. They would not miss that on the next time through. The ones who did not budge must have had Simonides (circa 500 B.C.), the father of the art of trained memory,[7] in their hip pockets!

We think too highly of ourselves when we do not think that we have to do the things that others do to achieve success. We think that our basic will is the panacea for all that would fall short in our music, or in business pursuits, or in our personal lives, or specifically, in the sight of God.

Marking our music teaches us a great deal about life. Music editors are great about putting in all of the little indicators like tempo, dynamics, crescendos, and so forth, but the editors cannot put everything onto the printed page that we will need to consider, nor can they anticipate what problems we will encounter along the way.

Use your pencil. It places fewer burdens on your memory, and you can count on it, just like a good, good friend, to be there for you the next time you pass that way again. Those marks you carefully place in your music will not lie to you. They are on your side. They want you to get it right.

*Push us. Pull us. Prompt us. In the name of the Word Made Flesh we pray,* AMEN.

# 11. Why Sing A Cappella?

*We will never figure out all of the intricacies of music.*
*Nevertheless, we can certainly try to get all from it that our minds*
*can absorb, and our spirits can reflect.*

As we construct our lives and our music, we, out of
necessity, must reach upward, working to improve after we
have paved a solid base.

*Therefore, let us go towards perfection, leaving behind the basic*
*teaching about Christ, and not laying again the*
*foundation: repentance from the dead works and faith towards*
*God.*
*~Hebrews 6:1*

When choirs sing *a cappella,* they put themselves on the line.
There is no hiding place in *a cappella* or unaccompanied
choral music. Singers must tune to each other and not to an
accompanying instrument. If a singer is out of tune or out of
place, the listeners will know. This kind of singing is the
hallmark of successful choirs. It is standard fare in
college/university choirs.

A *cappella* means *church style,* for it rose to prominence in
the Renaissance, as European composers learned to write
music that made choirs sound angelic and robust in their
lofty cathedrals, bouncing sound around walls of stone.
Most any singer who has ever sung this style of music in
such a house of worship, and sung it well, knows the joy and
satisfaction that such a performance gives. While singing, it
causes the performer to believe in the theory that the whole
is greater than sum of the individual parts. This synergetic
appeal is almost mysterious.

There are times when *a cappella* singing is not feasible.
Maybe the confidence level of the group is not sufficient to
support it. Perhaps the voice distribution is not evenly

weighted. In any event, most all choirs should experience what it is like to create beautiful unisons and harmonies out of thin air.

*In the name of the Good Shepherd we pray,* AMEN.

# 12. Why Do We Warm-Up?

*Whether you are singing or playing (even an instrument that requires no wind), the sounds begin with breathing in and breathing out. Interpreters of sound must, out of necessity, give notes life, or as they say in Hebrew, Ruah, the breath of God.*

Great news! As we humble ourselves before God, we shed our anxieties.

*Cast all your cares on Him, for He cares for you.*
*~1 Peter 5:7*

Just as an athlete stretches before practice or competition, so does the musician. This takes place, not out of custom or to waste time, but out of the need to get ready, physically and mentally, to deal with the music at hand. Singers' instruments are part of their bodies and, therefore, should get treatment as such. If the body is weak or ill, so is the voice. The body comes alive for the day and invites the voice (morning singing) to wake up too.

Instrumentalists have a double transformation. They have to get their physical bodies going. They have to cause their external instruments to wake up and warm up. Instrumentalists find, through warm up, if a pad is leaking, if a valve is sticking, or if the snare is on.

Church musicians have a need for a warm up of the heart too. It is a tough thing to come into a church rehearsal straight from the pressures of the business world, or of private practice, or from being around non-believers all day and move into the religious sphere of church and its music. Christians who make music for the Lord should feel like they are transitioning when they attend rehearsals, services, and concerts. They should have a desire to warm up their hearts so that they might give and receive blessings. This transition does not suggest that they live as one kind of person away from church and live as another when they get there. Just the opposite is true. Sensitive believers are those who understand their need to solidify their thoughts and actions so that their music making might have deeper value. Without that, singing or playing is just that –singing and playing.

How many times have we felt the need for a warm up? We have to crave the warm up. Otherwise, we go to church out of habit. Then, we enter His gates with no thanksgiving, no expectation, and no joy. We need to guard against such possibilities.

*In the name of the God-made-man, Jesus we pray, AMEN.*

# III. Elaborating Questions

*Church musicians ask questions that extend and stretch the import of what they find through music and worship. Reading between the lines, what do the intricacies of their elaborating questions mean?*

## Jesus asked Elaborating Questions:

- *What can make salt regain its taste once it has lost it? (Matthew)*
- *How can Satan cast out Satan? (Mark)*
- *Is it easier to say, "You are forgiven," or "Arise and Walk"? (Luke)*
- *Don't you believe that I am in the Father, and that He is in me? (John)*

# 13. Am I Too Old For This?

*I hope that when I am old, I will pick up an instrument that I have never played before, and learn to play a few of my favorite songs on it to the delight of as many of my children and grandchildren as I can muster for an impromptu concert.*

We do not have time to stop and count all of our blessings, but from time to time we should pause long enough to name as many as we can.

*So even to old age and grey hairs, O God, do not forsake me, until I proclaim your might to all the generations to come.*
*~Psalm 71:18*

I know what some of you are thinking. You are thinking that you have sung in your church choir for long enough and that it is time to "retire." I see you nodding your head. Shame on you!

Realistically, there comes a time when all of us needs to –has to –change routine. Health matters and the like interfere. There is no golden retirement watch for choir to our knowledge. When we sign on, it appears that, more or less, we are making a life commitment. That is the way it should be. We sing because we have something to share. It has been a heartfelt requirement through the years. Nothing has changed except you, a little bit. Be honest. When you worship from any other angle than the choir loft you feel like you are missing something. Right?

Maybe your knees do not work as well as they used to work. Maybe it is harder to drive at night or to maneuver from home to church and back again. Make your needs known. Consider what you contribute to your church. What you lack in spring and vigor fades as your years of sagely service become obvious. You inspire in a multiplicity of ways as you give of yourself to others.

So hang on for as long as you possibly can. Even if, and especially if you are already "retired," know that these can be your best years, "characterized by action, direction, and passion."[8] Let your companions have the honor of serving you. Have you not said the same thing about others when they have had issues? Continue in your blessings. Continue to be a blessing. You are not occupying a chair that anyone else wants or needs. It is yours.

*Keep us following You –all our days. In the name of the Rock of Ages we pray,* AMEN.

# 14. Can Anyone Translate?

*Opera frightens us. We fear that foreign language operas are telling us things that we really need to know. The fact is we probably already know the lessons that most operas are expressing. We just do not know we know them. Therefore, we have to ask someone, or read about what is going on with him or her in a particular scene. This alone is a grand reason for a justification of opera.*

A specific language came into use when the Persians wrote about the Jewish people. Apparently, one for those times was when as exiles, under the tutelage of Zerubbabel, they prepared to rebuild the temple.

*And in the days of Artaxerxes, Bishlam and Mithredath and Tabeel and the rest of their associates wrote to King Artaxerxes of Persia; the letter was written in Aramaic and translated.*
*~Ezra 4:7*

We readily accept non-English words like "Hosanna," or "Alleluia," or "Halleluiah" or even "Gloria in Excelsis Deo" at church. We have used these for so long that they are as comfortable as an old shoe. We even think of them as being standard to the English language. But let us look in on a choir rehearsal where the director has selected a song that has this recurring lyric: *Siyahamb' ekukhanyen kwenkhos, Siyahamba, hamba* (We are marching in the Light of God, We are marching, marching):
  Choir Member #1: What is this?
  Director: It is a song from South Africa.
  Choir Member #2: Let's send it back (*Ha, Ha, Ha*)
  Director: We can learn this very quickly.
  Choir Member #3: We can't learn this. It's not in English!
  Choir member #4: What does it mean?

Director: Look at the bottom of the first page. There you will find the English translation.

Choir Member #4: Well, let's just sing it in English, then.

Choir Member #2: Yeah, let's sing it in English.

Director: Come on, it will be fun. Besides, there are... only a few words to learn, and they repeat.

Choir Member #3: I have enough trouble with English (*Ha, Ha, Ha*).

Rarely do we stop to listen to ourselves. We are willing to give money so that the Gospel spreads throughout the world, but when we try to bring a part of that world into our home church experiences, we throw up walls of resistance.

*Begin a new work in us. In the name of our Dayspring From on High,* AMEN.

# 15. Can Listeners Understand You?

*Gladly, the cross-eyed bear....Andy walks with me; Andy talks with me....And if the devil doesn't like it he can sit on a tack, sit on a tack Tuesday.... Sleep in heavenly peas. Sleep in heavenly peas.*

All of the various dimensions of our spiritual temple come together to bring the fullness of God.

*I pray that you may have the power to comprehend, with all the saints, what is the breadth and length and height and depth.*
*~Ephesians 3:18*

Duke Ellington, in perhaps his most prescient observation of the human condition, said, "It don't mean a thing if it ain't got that swing." To which he added the profound words, "Doo-ah, Doo-ah, Doo-ah, Doo-ah, Doo-ah, Doo-ah." Putting this in terms that are applicable to the church singer, "It's just for the birds if you don't pronounce your words...Doo-ah, Doo-ah, etc..."

To ensure this understanding of text-put-to-tune, a few churches out there will include choral lyrics in their weekly bulletin or worship folder so that congregations will catch the message of the songs. A growing number of churches will project choral words onto large screens to accomplish the same result.

Singers want listeners to participate in their songs. When they hear the words, they begin to understand why composers write as they do, giving longer note values to certain words or syllables requiring emphasis while assigning shorter, unstressed nuances to words that are subservient.

When people –performers and listeners alike– do this correctly, the heart cements words to pitches and rhythms in ways that are difficult to divide. For example, think of these words. "Amazing grace, how sweet the sound..." You heard more than words. You heard a melody playing out in your head just as real as the words themselves. The notes do not validate choral words, but they do elevate them to places that are sacred to our experience as Christians.

Life is a search for meaning. Freud avowed that our primary drive in life is to obtain pleasure. In contrast, and in keeping with the prevalent feeling among Christians, Frankl[9] believed that our lives come into focus as we pursue the things that we find meaningful. Believers find such meaning, over and again, through the marriage of holy words and musical expressions that, because of clarity, reach the soul.

*Stir us to hear Your message. In the name of the Messenger of the Covenant we pray, AMEN.*

# 16. Did You Notice I Was Missing?

*What is a musician's job at church? To present words and melodies that spring from their hearts in hopes that they will find resonance in the hearts of others. The mission is to empty themselves with praise to God, so that they and others might be filled from on high.*

Paul tells his readers in the city of Philippi "to live is Christ, to die is gain," and he gives this encouragement:

*Only, live your life in a manner worthy of the gospel of Christ, so that, whether I come and see you or am absent and hear about you, I will know that you are standing firm in one spirit, striving side by side with one mind for the faith of the gospel.*
*~Philippians 1:27*

When choir members are going to be absent, they usually let someone know. It is a custom of courtesy. There are some absences, however, that escape prediction. When the one who is out at such times returns, it is not out of the ordinary to hear the words, "I'm back. Did you people miss me? Did you even realize I was not here?"

Every person wants recognition in some way and to some degree. Choir people want to feel that their contributions of talent benefit the groups with which they identify. So the people who want to know if their absences are noted are actually asking for a validation of their continued work with others. Words like, "I know I'm just a warm body" and "I just take up a chair" are code words for "Please tell me that I make a difference."

Happy to oblige, music leaders shower them with the assurance that things were not the same without them. Everyone smiles. The director is happy, because the singer-ringer-player has returned. The singer-ringer-player is happy to know that there is a value placed on their investment of talent.

Jesus spoke of looking for the one sheep that had gone astray. Finding that sheep was so important that the shepherd left 99 others to go in search of it. We know that the value of "one" is a precious commodity to the Good Shepherd. Therefore, so it is to church choirs. When the proverbial "one" is missing, the whole flock changes. When that one returns, there is great rejoicing.

*Search high and low for all of us. In the name of the Shepherd we pray, AMEN.*

# 17. Is It the Best We Can Do?

*Our music is more convincing at church when we have ideas about what we are saying. If we neglect to live the way we sing, then our music falls short of its intended goal. When we work to live up to the message brought to us by God, through Christ, with the power of the Holy Spirit, then music ushers us into a holy, earthly place. This then is but an appetizer of what is to come.*

The following Doxology, or brief hymn of praise, is Jude's beautiful conclusion to his epistle, a work probably written shortly after the destruction of Jerusalem.

*To the only God our Savior, through Jesus Christ our Lord, be glory, majesty, power, and authority, before all time and now and forever.*
*~Jude 1:25*

The church wants to be cool and entertaining, so it builds a roller coaster inside its hall of worship. *Is that the best we can do?* The choir wants new members, so $20 bills are taped underneath "lucky" choir chairs to encourage attendance and growth. *Is that the best we can do?* The music minister wants to throw away the hymnals and religious songs written more than 25 years ago, because they do not -cannot speak to the contemporary heart. *Is that the best we can do?* The congregation closes, locks, and allows its pipe organ to collect dust because it wants to purchase an electronic keyboard that can modulate to any key at the touch of a button. *Is that the best we can do?* The pastor wants the choir out, and praise teams in, so some from the choir audition for the praise team with no other musical outlet left for choice. *Is that the best we can do?* The committee on worship wants everyone to dress casually at church. This makes those who want to wear suits and dresses feel "stuffy" and out of place. *Is that the best we can do?* The church faction wants to do away with traditional services so that, in the faction's words, "the church can grow." *Is that the best we can do?* The community churches want to have an ecumenical service on the Sunday evening before a major holiday. A church says that it cannot participate because it cannot call off it own service. *Is that the best we can do?* Standing on solid principles of the Word of God, shying away from game playing, respecting healthy traditions, utilizing all our resources of people and things, and casting Jesus' love in darkened places...*that is about the best we can do!*

*Replace our foolish ideas with those wise and holy ones that only You can supply. In the name of the Alpha and Omega we pray,* AMEN.

# 18. How Did We Do?

*There are times when we are much better than our music. Sadly, there are times when our music is much better than we are.*

God's love magnifies as He reasserts His unconditional love for His own. His grace extends beyond the rebellion of the chosen people.

*How can I give you up, Ephraim? How can I hand you over,*
*O Israel? How can I make you like Admah?*
*How can I treat you like Zeboiim? My heart recoils within me;*
*my compassion grows warm and tender.*
*~Hosea 11:8*

Music exists at different levels. One level is its presentation. "How did that sound," we ask. Another level is conceivably more subjective than the first when we ask, "How did we do?" *How did we do* is more about how we feel about ourselves in relation to the message or emotion we proclaim. *How did we do* asks how, or if, the music has changed us.

There is no suggestion here that music, in and of itself, has the power to change people. Music, after all, is just music. It is just notes, connected to rhythms, connected to harmonies, connected to feelings. The power of suggestion comes when a song comes to mind, and you can listen to it, under the banner of that name, and find images or moods swinging around between the ears.

The *aha* comes when music marries words. Such a marriage conveys specific impressions about whatever the composer wishes to express. Think of instrumental music. If that music has an association with a text you know, you will find yourself thinking of the words as you hear the musical sounds. If the song is unknown to you, you think of it in a completely different manner. You feel the power of suggestion of moods as the music plays itself along.

*Be for us what we cannot be for ourselves. In the name of the Great 'I Am" we pray,* AMEN.

# IV. Divergent Questions

*Church musicians use prior knowledge as a platform from which to kick-off to other questions, much like a swimmer uses the end of the pool to propel away again when making a turn.*

<u>*Jesus asked Divergent Questions:*</u>

- *Why do we see faults in others but not in ourselves? (Matthew)*
- *Is it lawful to do good on the Sabbath days? (Mark)*
- *Are not five sparrows sold for two farthings? (Luke)*
- *If you do not believe Moses' writings, why believe his words? (John)*

# 19.  Is She Willing to Audition?

*There are occasions when music is so beautiful that it makes us a little bit uncomfortable. We remember these times long after the music stops.*

The Bible records that none of young Samuel's words "fell on the ground." In other words, when he spoke, people listened, because he had something worthy to say.

*And all Israel from Dan to Beer-Sheba knew that Samuel was a trustworthy prophet of the LORD.*
*~1 Samuel 3:20*

A few choirs hold membership auditions. Those choirs tend to be the ones that have a plethora of resources that allow them the luxury of *cherry picking* those who will fill key slots in their choral groups and instrumental ensembles. Such is not the case for the vast majority of church choirs. "We are looking for warm bodies," choir members will openly declare.

At some point, however, talent has to factor into the church music equation. Solos pop up. Who will sing them? Does the director assign solos (a practice that lends itself to "She always gets picked" or "He is the only one willing to do it")? On the other hand, does the director call for try-outs (a practice that causes the entire back row of the choir loft to tremble with anticipation)?

Either way, the deal making starts. "I will sing it if she can sing it with me." Before the director can respond, another voice says, "Let's just let everyone do it. We don't have to make that a solo anyway."

Auditions conjure up the business of being *good enough* to do what we do in church music. Of course, no one of us is good enough to deserve the blessings that are ours, but when we mention an *audition*, it places a spotlight squarely on us. We face the reality that most of us are never going to audition for anything. As content as we are in church choir, if it means that we must undergo some kind of scorecard, no thank you.

Trust your inner voice. That voice is telling you if an audition, should it ever come your way, is right for you. We contribute in a variety of ways. Know what your contribution is, and be happy with yourself.

*Cause us to examine ourselves and to give thanks for gifts unspeakable. In the name of the Sun of Righteousness we pray,*
AMEN.

# 20. Can We Have An Extra Practice?

*Let us face it. Music is profound. It is deep. It is serious. It requires
us to approach it as players and as listeners with rigorous intent.
Otherwise, we will gain little or no joy from it.*

Azariah, the High Priest, once exhorted his people to keep
their chins up by remembering the benefits that come with
keeping faith alive. How timely this is for us to hear again.

*But you, take courage! Do not let your hands be weak, for your
work shall be rewarded.*
*~2 Chronicles 15:7*

It happens as one of your big performances draws near. You
know those special music services that your choir leads from
time to time. Sometimes a hand will go up. An adult, in
rather childlike innocence will wait his turn, and the
question comes, just as the director knew it would: "Would
it be possible for us to have a bonus rehearsal before we do
this?" Seconds and thirds to the motion gather from across
the choral ranks. The request seems to be open for
discussion.

Why is it that the people who attend the least percentage
of rehearsals are typically the ones who, with the question of
an added practice, insinuate benignly that the director has
neglected to teach them their music? Why is it that those
most distracted by life are the last ones in choirs to come to
terms with their parts? You reach the point where you will
take commitment over talent any day of the week...and twice
on Sunday.

A person does not have to attend choir practice –or even
church for that matter—to have a vital relationship with
Lord, but we are not talking about that here. We are not
talking about individual preparedness. Quite the contrary is
at work. Choir is a melding process whereby the

contributions of the singular person go out to all in hopes that multiple voices work together as one.

Therefore, if it means that a call for extra practice happens, then it should happen. Those who need it the most need it the most.

*Work with us. Work in us. Work through us. Work in spite of us. In the name of our Unspeakable Gift we pray, AMEN.*

# 21. Do You Remember...?

*Music and memory are twins, separated at birth and almost reunited from time to time.*

Our days are numbered. Our time is limited. Let us make the most of our opportunities.

*I think it right, as long as I am in this body, to refresh your memory.*
*~2 Peter 1:13*

We lack the capacity to remember many important things from our past. Some things we have purposefully deleted long ago, for they just took up too much space on our hard drives. Some things, though, we wish we could remember in exquisite detail, but they will not surface. They languish in the windmills of our minds.

Enter the power of music: Why is it that when we hear certain songs we fly, at warp speed, back to the times and places when we played, danced to, or sang these songs?

Church choir people need to develop a repertoire of musical memory. Think of the thousands of pitches that choirs hoist and instrumental people raise. It is impossible to remember them all. Some will stand out, and they should, for these flowed when a special person passed away, married, was baptized, or received redemption. There are those that have spoken to us at pivotal times when we really needed to hear certain messages from God. These notes had medicinal properties for our souls, and as such, they linger now and will never leave us.

Such music becomes aural photographs. We see them. They become 3-D. We feel them. They become spirit food. We taste them. They become for us a part of the fabric of our being. We wear them.

This happens for individuals all of the time. Once in a great while, this happens to a group, and the group has the same group experience as has already been described for individuals. When this happens, it is like that rare comet streaking across the sky. You had to see it. You had to trace its path. You had to be there. No one else will ever understand.

*Rekindle our spirits. In the name of He Who Is All Wisdom,*
AMEN.

# 22. Have We Already Sung This?

*All music is heart music, or at least it should be. That is where it should begin and end.*

We need to practice obedience to God's ways. When we fail to do this, our lives spin out of control.

*Now we command you, beloved, in the name of our Lord Jesus Christ, to keep away from believers who are living in idleness and not according to the tradition that they received from us.*
*~2 Thessalonians 3:6*

If you direct church choirs, you never know if the question, "have we sung this before?" is a good question or a bad one. It could mean, "Wow! I know we have sung this one before, and I am so glad to be singing it again." Alternatively, it could mean, "I remember this one. I hated it the last time around, and I'm sure I will hate it this time too." The director usually makes the assumption that the singer innocently and genuinely does not remember singing it before and that the question is not a loaded one.

It is more than acceptable to repeat music. After all, the congregation does it all the time. We would never take the position that, just because we sang the congregation's favorite hymn this year that we cannot repeat it ever or at least not for a long time to come. Choirs love certain songs. Usually they wind up loving the ones they make sound the best. They like the ones they know the best. It is much easier to say, "Let's sing *such and such* this Sunday, we already know it," than it is to learn new music material.

Scripture says to sing a new song.

We can fulfill that scripture when we take old songs and learn them anew when we return to them. If we are sensitive musicians, we can find new things in the songs that we did not realize were there on previous exposures to them. Old songs are new when we see them with fresh eyes and hear them with fresh ears. If we sing them this way, our congregations will hear them this way.

*Speak to our hearts, Lord Jesus. In the name of the Creator we pray,* AMEN.

# 23. Is That in His Key?

*Is music good? Is music bad? Music cannot be either one. It can only be what we ascribe to it.*

Jesus' own work is crowned in those who seek His will and do His work.

*We will make you ornaments of gold, studded with silver.*
*~Song of Songs 1:11*

We need to find the right song in life. Blest is the person who finds it. Once we place our arms around it, we need to get it in our key. Blest is the person who can modulate. After we get the key adjusted to fit our high and low notes, we must rehearse our song. Blest is the person who works hard at it. When the song is ready, it needs an audience. Blest is the person who has some listeners. Following its airing, the song is sure to draw comments of praise or criticism. Blest is the person who can discount the good and upgrade the bad. In response to the feedback, we need to refine what we can with the song. Blest is the person who can take a simple tune and make it profoundly original.

For musicians, there are musical experiences that are misleading. When it might seem that we will not find success in them, we try them in another key. That is when we meet exhilaration hard to describe. The song that eluded us now becomes a friend. The song we did not like is now the song we cannot stop singing.

We cannot help but tell others about the song, how we found it, and how it did not change but how it discovered a way to find us where we were, in a place ready to receive it. That song becomes like an "ornament of gold, studded with silver," crowning our days with its beauty and its omnipresence. May God be praised!

*Breathe Your sweet song into our receptive ears. In the name of the One Who Is Crowned With Many Crowns,* AMEN.

# 24. Where is the Coda?

*Descending or ascending notes, if continued, will eventually get to the place where we cannot hear them anymore. However, that does not mean that they are not there, doing their work.*

David's vision for the Temple was so vivid that he could speak about it in colorful detail. His instructions to his son and successor, Solomon, revealed that his own tastes did not guide him and that he respected, out of fear, the instructions he had received from the Lord.

*All this, in writing at the Lord's direction, he made clear to me –*
*the plan of all the works.*
*~1 Chronicles 28:19*

It is hard enough, sometimes, to keep up with the music. Maybe the tempo races along or there are so many words that it is easy to get behind, or ahead of, the true beat. Then there are those repeat signs. Just when you find out where everyone else is singing, it is time to go back and sing the section you just missed a second time. *If it got away from me the first time, why do I think there will be a different outcome on the next pass?*

Look for the sign. S-i-g-n, which uses the same letters as s-i-n-g, but in a slightly different order. Terms like *D.S.* and *Fine* inform us where to go and when to stop.

When you read music, you know what the signs are. When you do not, and many faithful choir members do not, you have to write notes to yourself in the music. Words like, *Go back to measure 5* or *repeat this line* or *jump to the coda on the second line of page 6* creep in to the margins of the printed music.

This is another place where being in church choir and negotiating the dictates of musical performance serves a more esoteric purpose in our lives, for when we know where we are, where we are going, and what to do when we get there, we are healthier, happier, and more adjusted. Christians know that the Bible holds keys that unlock doors of opportunity for us to mature and develop as people. Few of us, however, actually map out our lives on paper, in an authentic master plan of empowering and inspiring exercises[10] in the same way that the music editor charts the course of a musical performance on the printed page. We do not get lost as often, or when we do, we find our way back to the intended course with greater speed and accuracy.

*Light our paths. In the name of Our Lamp we pray,* AMEN.

# V. Subsidiary Questions

*Church musicians pose subsidiary questions. These are helpful, for they combine to help build answers to essential questions.*

<u>*Jesus asked Subsidiary Questions:*</u>

- *Do you understand what my parables mean? (Matthew)*
- *Do you err because you do not know the power of God? (Mark)*
- *Was my baptism from John or from heaven? (Luke)*
- *Do you believe me? (John)*

# 25. Do We Have a Sunshine Fund?

*God wants us to love one another. Nothing reminds us of this fact more than music.*

We know that the heat of the sun and the dews of the night both serve vital functions in ripening produce.

*For thus the Lord said to me: I will quietly look for my dwelling like clear heat in sunshine, like a cloud of dew in the heat of harvest.*
*~Isaiah 18:4*

Church musicians undergo operations, hospital stays, periods of bereavement, new birth, death, and accidents. Many choirs find it advantageous to pass the hat once a month or so to accumulate money, often referred to as a "Sunshine Fund." This fund allows the choir, with ease, to respond to extraordinary events that come the way of its members. Usually the outreach comes in the form of a flower arrangement or a choir-signed card or a meal delivery. Rarely do these funds relate to happy events that do not require medical care. Marriages, anniversaries, birthdays and things of that nature usually work in other ways.

There are funds that respond only to choir member situations. There are funds that include choir spouses and choir children. There are funds that include choir spouses, children, parents, uncles, aunts, cousins...*ad nauseam*. There is no right or wrong way to do this. The fact that a choir wants to do something like this, and so many do, speaks volumes, for you see it is impossible (except in opera) to fight, be contentious, or selfish when you make music with others.

Jesus loves us. We know this. The Bible tells us. That is why giving to those we love in times of pain and struggle fits into the patterns forged by Christian pilgrims.

Alexandre Dumas' *Three Musketeers* confidently recited the mantra, *all for one and one for all*, at times when they needed to pull together. Christian musicians know that Jesus is the *One* who gave and gives Himself for all. We want be imitators of Him.

*Send us swiftly to others. In the name of the Advocate we pray,*
AMEN.

# 26. Can We Make That a Solo?

*Do you believe that every person has a song, in the metaphorical sense? If you do believe this, then what are you doing about your song? If you do not believe this, then why do you not?*

No effective church vocal or instrumental soloist would ever dream of being the center of attention. The message of their music always takes supremacy over their personal, unique gifts.

*The haughtiness of people shall be humbled, and the pride of everyone shall be brought low; and the Lord alone will be exalted on that day.*
*~Isaiah 2:17*

Choir people want the easy way out. We all do, right? When church choir people work a piece of music that causes them concern that they might have to put forth a little, or a lot more effort to "pull it off," they begin to think of clever ways to get out of it. One of the most ingenious methods is the suggestion that a portion of the song, or the entire song, passes off to someone with more talent –to someone for whom the song would be easy. "Can we make this one a solo?" This maneuver reminds us of the old Life Cereal commercial where the bowl of suspicious breakfast passes over to little brother, Mikey, who "eats everything." Mikey becomes the lab rat who experiments to see if those toasted whole grains (musical notes) are going to harm us if we actually ingest (sing) them. If you are too young to remember that commercial, ask an elder or consult your online video sources.

Most of us in-the-shower soloists are not soloists at all when you get right down to it. We dream dreams about this and that, never really doing any of the things that would be necessary to inch us closer to fulfilling those dreams. Church solos become a metaphor for the fulfillment of personal interests. We have to identify the song we are to sing. We have to learn it. We have to gather enough courage to try it aloud. We have to practice. We have to set a date and time for its performance. Moreover, and most importantly, *we* have to do it. After that, it exists in memory as a do-over or as a thing that we chalk up to experience.

So, before you volunteer someone else to sing a solo, ask yourself if the song is really yours.

*Sing through our desires. In the name of the Bishop of Souls we pray, AMEN.*

# 27. Are You Sure You Want Me?

*If you are to use the gifts you have, or cultivate those you need to improve for God in musical ways, then you have the guarantee that you will be a little uncomfortable until you do what you know you need to do.*

We all have particular things and people that cause us happiness. Find your happiness producers as soon as you can, and hold them fast.

*Hope deferred makes the heart sick, but a desire fulfilled is a tree of life.*
*~Proverbs 13:12*

Most church choir people are recruiters at heart. They are talent merchants. They pounce on opportunities to get additional people to join in church music making. If you doubt this, check out the first person to greet a visitor in worship. "Are you musical?" the director will ask. This question, quite often, comes before a formal introduction.

"Are you sure you want me in choir?" The conversation usually continues this way. The potential singers will add, "After all, I don't read music." Some will insert a joke as a way of making their point. "I really can't carry a tune in a bucket!"

It never hurts to ask. People do not get their feelings hurt when they are invited to choir. Some, frequently those rare few who truly cannot "carry" that tune, will use the invitation as a source of pride, openly recounting the invitation to as many people as possible whenever the subject of church music surfaces. "They don't want *me* up there" (profuse laughter).

At other times, the loving spouse volunteers the news as they greet each new music director. "I told (insert director's name here) the choir did not need (insert non-singer's name here)." People want to feel needed, and they want someone to hear them. It seems as if half of the people are forever complaining about the other half not listening to them. We need to work at developing new techniques for becoming better listeners.[11]

Then there are those who are just waiting for an invitation. Privately, they have dreamed about being in the choir. They have heard the fruits of choral labor, and it has sounded like a magnificent adventure to them. However, they stand back, for reasons that reflect their personalities, and wait for that official invitation to do the very thing for which they should be volunteering.

In their hearts, they are already there.

*Provide the courage for us to be a part and not apart. In the name of the Heir of All Things we pray, AMEN.*

# 28. Did Someone Hurt Her Feelings?

*Music provides a great escape for those who grow weary from life. It is like medicine.*

Sometimes we have to press on, even when we do not feel like it. May our conflicts be from without rather than from within.

*But though we had already suffered and been shamefully maltreated at Philippi, as you know, we had courage in our God to declare to you the gospel of God in spite of great opposition.*
*~1 Thessalonians 2:2*

Minister of Music: Someone hurt her feelings.

Pastor: I didn't hurt her feelings. Did you?

Minister of Music: No. I thought that maybe you had.

Pastor: I don't know anything about it.

Minister of Music: Some choir people told me about it. That's how I came to find out.

Pastor: Why are people always getting their feelings bruised at church?

Minister of Music: I don't know. But you have to be ready for it to crop up at any time.

Pastor: Are you going to talk to her?

Minister of Music: I already tried. She won't say what the real problem is. She just says that she's not coming back. Ever.

Pastor: Do you think I should visit her at her home?

Minister of Music: You could try, but I don't think it would do much good. She says to remove her name from the choir roster.

Pastor: She'll come around.

Administrative Assistant: You have a call holding.

Pastor: Thanks, Margaret.

Minister of Music: I'll talk to you later, after things cool off.

This interchange is about the pastor's five-year-old granddaughter in the church preschool area.

*Correct us when we are wrong. In the name of the Deliverer we pray,* AMEN.

# 29. Will You Talk to Her?

*What would happen if we could read people the way we read music? Would we be able to teach more? To learn more? Alternatively, by taking all of the marvelous guesswork out of the equation, would life become more dull and dreary?*

The work of the Lord is perfect. Ours is not.

*Now may our Lord Jesus Christ Himself and God our Father, who loved us and through grace gave us eternal comfort and good hope, comfort your hearts and strengthen them in every good work and word.*
*~2 Thessalonians 2:16-17.*

She is a problem. She has been a problem since she joined the choir. She makes out of turn comments in rehearsals. She thinks she is funny, but she is sadly mistaken. She hurts people's feelings. She laughs at the wrong times. You can smell her before she hits the choir room door –too much perfume in an attempt to cover the telltale aroma of tobacco. Rumor has it, her breath smells of alcohol most of the time. You need to talk to her.

What are you going to say? Will you say that nobody likes her? Will you say that she should stay away from us? Will you say she does not need you? Will you say that her odor offends? Will you ask her if she is an alcoholic? Tread carefully here, for this is where you can have a real ministry.

You see, she loves her identification with your choir more than just about anything in the world. Her love for music and the Lord have brought her to you. Many of her needs are filled at church in spite of the fact that her presence is bringing down *esprit de corps*.

You say to her the things that God would have you say, and you say them in love and with another person or two who score high on the empathy scale. You do not ignore, and you do not seek to offend. You try to help. It is a part of your duty as a Christian.

Maybe she gets upset and leaves the church. Maybe she does not. Either way you have done what you should do. Either way, you let her know that there is a welcome for her that comes from the Lord and those who will try to be her friends.

*Bring power and insight. In the name of Our Great Prophet we pray,* AMEN.

# 30. Can She Sing?

*Most of us know what we like and like what we know. Sadly, that does not leave much room for new things.*

Most of us are much more prone to open our mouths than to open our eyes or ears. We need to live so that we might influence others for God.

*For it is God's will that by doing right you should silence the ignorance of the foolish.*
*~1 Peter 2:15*

Most people who can sing know they can sing. Most people who cannot sing know they cannot sing. Some people, heaven help us, cannot sing, but they lack any clue that they cannot sing. We shall consider this issue for just a minute or two together.

People who cannot sing...Is there no place for them in the Kingdom? Of course there is. Why are these people so sweet? Why is it that they are well intentioned in spite of the fact that their vocal machinery is not. If these people were jerks, it would be so easy to say, "Hey, you sound like a banshee when you sing. Make like a banana and *split*. Make like a tree and *leaf*!

God does not judge us, thankfully, by the quality of our song. We receive worth through our willingness to be a song. Believers should find places that allow for the successful outpouring of gifts. These are sacrifices of praise to the Lord. Such gifts, nobly offered and divinely received, please God and humankind.

Back to the non-singer singer...The people around them had better be secure in their own singing, or they will veer off track by the non-singers' bleating tones. Should they leave choir? Probably not. Directors should find ways to work with them, preferably at times other than formal rehearsals, to equip them with the awareness that what they are doing does not resemble what others are doing. When they can hear themselves as others hear them, they will begin to improve vocally or begin to consider other ways to reflect God's grace to others.

*Smooth our rough edges. In the name of the One True God we pray,* AMEN.

# VI. Probing Questions

*Church musicians want to get below the surface of issues in order to get to the most important aspects of them.*

<u>*Jesus asked Probing Questions:*</u>

- *What good is it to love only those who love you? (Matthew)*
- *By what authority do I do these things? (Mark)*
- *Don't you count the cost before you build? (Luke)*
- *For which of my good works do you stone me? (John)*

# 31. Can You Hear Each Other?

*Music allows us to let notes and rhythms think on our behalf.*

Jesus loved to tell stories. As it turns out, stories serve as a brilliant pedagogy for making a point. When Jesus told a story, He knew what He was doing and why He was doing it.

*The reason I speak to them in parables is that "seeing they do not perceive, and hearing they do not listen, nor do they understand."*
*~Matthew 13:13*

What is that sound, that to my ear
Brings joy, delight to what I hear?
What is that whispered voice, that to my core
Is loud and clear?

It is the Spirit, Holy, true
That gives me strength for what I do.
It is the wind and fire of grace
That works within, without, and through.

I can place your voice with mine.
We can sing the songs divine,
But you and I together cannot hold
All of the sounds on which the angels dine.

Every sister, every brother,
Every sameness, every *other*
Knows that as we partner in Christ-like dance
We must give-take, one way or another.
For when we know each other's part,
Only then can music start
To fill us in on what we've missed
By weight of heart.

Raise your hands as music sweet
Brings down glory, head to feet.
Many gifts unite as one
As diverse paths from mercy meet.

*Send us to each other. In the name of the Peacemaker we pray,*
AMEN.

# 32. Can You Hear the Piano?

*You do not usually hum a harmony. You hum a melody. That is how much weight it holds.*

There was a time when Israel, for its sins, found itself in captivity.

*They would not listen, however, but they continued to practice their former custom.*
*~2 Kings 17:40*

The impressive piano can cover a bunch of choral sins. Take, for instance, those songs that have the words "accompaniment optional" inserted at the beginning. Most choirs, especially the small ones, might as well take pen to hand and mark out the word "optional" and in its place spell out the word "r-e-q-u-i-r-e-d." Usually the accompaniment in these songs mirrors the same notes that the choir performs, so playing the accompaniment is redundant. The music makes its case without it.

That "required" piano does more than "sing" the notes that choirs should be singing. It has the marvelous ability to sing "in tune" at times when voices alone might drop or float sharp. In that capacity, the piano is more than a voice, it takes on the role of a surveyor, marking out where the property line of one part ends and another begins. It helps to keep choral neighbors at home and off the turf of others.

Pianos can pull off a feat that eludes the human voice –it can, in the right hands –play (sing) all of the parts at the same time. Whereas people, physiologically, can manage only one sound at a time, pianos know no such restraint. A piano can multi-task with the best of them.

When a piano accompanies a choir, the singers ought to listen to it, because it is there to serve, not to compete. It possesses the message of embellishment, using all that it can to add to the communication of the text. The piano's role is complementary, for it cannot speak words. It has no soul. It must have people to play it or sing with it to give it ephemeral life.

*Accompany us in our going out and in our coming in. In the name of the Most Blessed Forever we pray,* AMEN.

# 33. Can You See the Beat?

*When we hear, the effect is for but for a moment. When we listen, the effect is for a much longer bit of time.*

When Moses had been in the presence of the Lord, his face reflected God's glory. Therefore, we need to shine when we experience personal encounters with the Lord.

*And all of us, with unveiled faces, seeing the glory of the Lord as though reflected in a mirror, are being transformed into the same image from one degree of glory to another; for this comes from the Lord, the Spirit.*
*~2 Corinthians 3:18*

A conductor is as essential to a performance at church as the crossing guard is to the boys and girls who walk busy streets on their way to and from their elementary schools. Great conductors are those who have the ability to become invisible and let the performers do all of the talking during times of performance. Conductors are far from being silent creatures, though. It begs saying that conductors have much to talk about during periods of rehearsal that lead to their performances. Conductors are mute when the music shines. They make no music. In their purest sense, they do not even respond to music. They anticipate it. They hear it in their heads, and they do their best to convince others to hear it the way they do.

Someone somewhere joked that a musical conductor only needs to know two things: 1) What the music should sound like, and 2) What to do to cause musicians to sound it that way.

If it were easy, it would be easy! A conductor has a special seat –you might say the very best seat in the house – from which to soak in all of the music that comes out of a group of performers. From this perch, the conductor oversees the work of numerous parts and sections that fit together to form musical opuses short and long, easy and challenging.

Conductors tend to insist on their own way. Does this mean that they are dictatorial, micro managing, or downright mean? Sometimes. However, most often, conductors are those hard-working people who want to usher the musicians with whom they share life and sound to places that lie just beyond their reach. It does not get much better than that, especially for church people.

*Watch over us, and watch us as we look to You. In the name of the Bright and Morning Star we pray, AMEN.*

# 34. Who Will Lead Us?

*A real leader faces the music, even when she/he does not like the tune.*

Joel observed the militaristic order of the swarming phase of the short-horned grasshopper –the locust. He saw that, without a leader, they were able to move forth in perfect precision.

*Like warriors they charge, like soldiers they scale the wall. Each keeps to its own course. They do not swerve from their paths.*
*~Joel 2:7*

In most churches, there is usually a person who is the go-to person about the music. In congregations of any dimension, one person is responsible for selecting, preparing, and presenting music for the activities of church life. When churches are in need of a leader, they need to ask themselves where they have been, where they are, and where they want to go as a worshiping people. This kind of discernment will guide them down appropriate paths toward a special local or imported person who will journey with them. After all, a church is not trying to fill a spot on the church staff; a church is trying to fill a need. Musicians may be plentiful, but the church needs to feel that there is that one, special person who is the perfect fit for the needs and desires of the church.

Once the person comes, the church and the musician need to enter into a covenant relationship. The church is there to support its music leader. The music leader is there to uplift the Lord and to contribute to life with the people of the church. Prayer support needs offering. What is good for the church should be good for the musician. What is good for the musician should be good for the church. It will take resources of people, money, and time to do the job.

The musician should work to growth in faith and in the practice of church music. This is not an easy task, for to be a great leader, you have to work hard at it every day.[12] Some music leaders receive payment for their work. Others do not. Under whatever terms the church music leaders serve, their churches need to respect their opinions and value their giftedness. As the church changes, so will its music leader. The church and the leader need to stay connected, and communicate mission, message, and the most effective ways of using music to accomplish those things.

*In the name of the Savior we pray,* AMEN.

# 35. Will You Sing It For Us?

*Some people come into this world with amazing talent. Others, the real lucky ones, figure out how to use their talents to the fullest.*

God does not need our worship in order to be, or to remain, God. We know, through scripture, to offer sacrifices that come from our hearts. God desires our praise and is the worthy recipient of them.

*Call on me in the day of trouble; I will deliver you, and you shall glorify me.*
*~Psalm 50:15*

"We can't get that part at the top of page four. Will you sing it for us?" the frustrated woman on the end of the second row blurted out. This kind of musical problem teaches us about life. There are occasions when we want to see a pattern so we will know what the product of something will look like. In church choir, we like to hear someone sing a difficult measure, the right way, so we can adjust our individual sounds to match what the music asks of us.

A trained singer who reads music very well can sing our parts for us the way they are supposed to be sung; but, in the end, we have to sing them for ourselves. That is Christian life. We can admire Christian friends, but we have to be imitators of Christ for ourselves. We seek to grow in our faith. We seek to grow in our musicianship. What does it say about the singers who knew nothing about music when they joined the church choir 27 years ago and who know nothing more about it now than  they did then? What does it say about the person who picks up the occasional something about music, applying that knowledge to each subsequent musical rehearsal and performance?

Let us face it. Some of us are not God's gift to music. Some of us feel much more confident about musical faith when singers, possessing extraordinary gifts, surround us. In choir, and in life, we need to huddle close. Those troublesome phrases are on the next page.

We all could use a little nudge from time to time. Show me where we are in the music –Where are we? When is it time for our entrance? Is she going to give us a cut-off at bar 19? We want to know. We want to do it right. We want to live it right.

*In the name of the God of Abraham, Isaac, and Jacob we pray,*
AMEN.

# 36. Would You Cue Us There?

*If life is a game of billiards, and you are the cue ball, then you are definitely going to be in the game.*

The worshiping bodies of the Old and New Testaments become one in triumph as the songs of deliverance from bondage blend with the songs of praise to the Lamb of God. What a beautiful mental image!

*And they sing the song of Moses, the servant of God, and the song of the Lamb: Great and amazing are your deeds, Lord God the Almighty!*
*~Revelation 15:3*

"Will you cue us there?" Jimmy asked. Really, his question sounded more like a command, like "You *will* cue us there." Conductors work to improve their conducting. At least they should. Musicians rely on the director, the central figure, to get things started, to keep things together, and to make adjustments in tempo, dynamics, and much, much more.

Jimmy's question (uh, strong suggestion) is well placed. Performers need to let their leaders know where they are having trouble with the music. Some conductors focus on one part or another and fail to realize what they are asking of a particular section. Conductors should try, whenever possible, to experience music as the performers do. Often, performers see it from the trenches. That can be a very different terrain from the director's lay of the land on the podium.

Communication is essential to establishing good life relationships and good music. Much of that communication is non-verbal in music. Through gestures, much happens from the director to the ensemble. Each has a responsibility to keep the communication flowing in multiple directions – between director and musician, between musician and director, between musician and musician, and between musician, conductor, and accompanying instruments.

For a moment, think of Peter. When he kept his eyes on the Lord, he had no trouble walking on water, but when he thought he had that task mastered, he transferred his gaze. He lost his lifeline and his rudder. Sinking like a rock, he knew that his hydroplaning days were over. Musicians, lost in a score, know that feeling.

Directors, cue your people on everything you can as many times as you can. Performers, get in the habit of watching. When directors demand more from their people and when people demand more from their directors, better experiences with music result. Remember, none of us should feel that we are out on the rough seas alone.

*In the name of He who traveled from and to heaven,* AMEN.

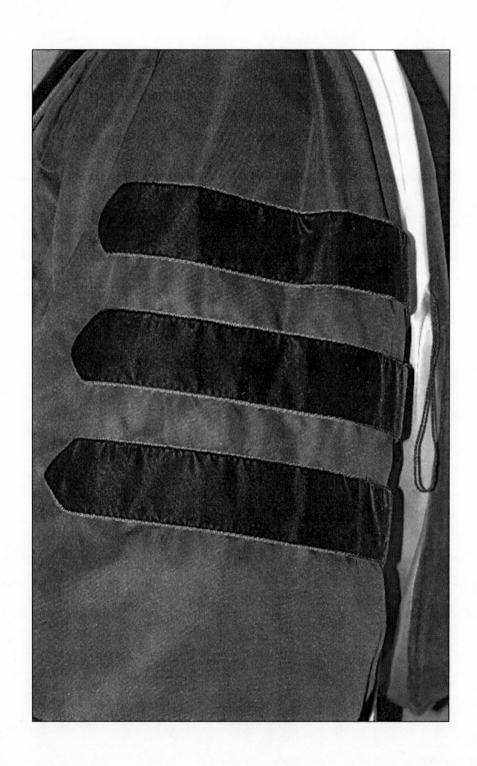

# VII. Unanswerable Questions

*Church musicians want to challenge themselves by asking questions that are difficult to answer.*

<u>Jesus asked Unanswerable Questions:</u>

- *Why are you standing here doing nothing? (Matthew)*
- *How is it that you have no faith? (Mark)*
- *Why do you call me Lord and fail to do the things I say? (Luke)*
- *Are there not twelve hours in the day? (John)*

# 37. Are There Any More Copies of This?

*As beautiful as music can be, so potentially ugly is the business
that surrounds music.*

Recorded in Esther is an account of a terrible decree. It went
out, by means of runners, throughout the land and in all
languages.

*A copy of the document was to be issued as a decree in every
province by proclamation, calling on all the peoples to be ready for
that day.*
*~Esther 3:14*

When distributing music at a church rehearsal, it is easy to
think of grilling hamburgers. What? Grilling, you say?

When distributing music at a church choir rehearsal, it is
easy to think of shrinkage. Oh, now it makes more sense. Do
go on.

For some inexplicable reason, when $x$ number of copies
of music are purchased, stamped, carded, computer-fielded,
or otherwise catalogued, $y$ number of copies are available
when it time to hand out a title, particularly a new title.

Seasoned grillers, *uh*, directors know that to have
enough copies of music you must buy more than enough.
The formula is quite simple. Take the average number of
singers who have attended rehearsals over the previous 12-
month period. Divide that number by the average number of
singers who have come to worship over the same number of
months. Subtract the number of Mondays that it rained
during the previous April, add the total number of minutes
in your pastor's typical sermon.... you get the drift.

While it is hard to know where it all goes when you
need it, it is so startling to find copies everywhere once the
song has been used in worship and has been tucked away,
back in the secret places where church music is stored.

The church is a great proving ground for legal compliance. When there is a need for additional copies of the music, honest churches go out and buy them.

The copier in the church office is not equipped to handle requests for more copies; however, all of you know that already.

When it comes to church music, make mine well done.

*Stay with us, and keep our numbers sufficient. In the name of the Image of God we pray,* AMEN.

# 38. Do the Men Sing There?

*There are only twelve pitches in our scale. That is all. Therefore, there is nothing to writing and performing music. You only have twelve things from which to choose.*

The Israelites had entered into an unholy alliance with another tribe after God had expressly forbidden it.

*Therefore, the leaders partook of their provisions, and did not ask direction from the Lord.*
*~Joshua 9:14*

Quite often, a church choir populates with people who do not read music. These people rely on placing their radar on the music readers around them. Most of these non-readers are people who have pleasant voices. They need support from musically literate friends. "Do the men sing there?" a common question, is sincere. The questioner can read words, so any editorial comments written in the music make perfect sense. The question is deeper, for that singer knows the director periodically alters the music to fit needs of balance and blend and to prop up vocal lines that may suffer because of member absences. The questioner is after accuracy, a most worthy goal.

It is not rude to ask questions in a choral or instrumental rehearsal. Clarity arrives as people draw together through consensus about how the music is supposed to come to life. It is not a sign of ignorance to ask questions in a choral or instrumental rehearsal. Many times, the person who knows the most knows how to dig to draw even more vitality from the printed page. To question is not just a woman thing or a man thing, although the joke, *Why did Moses wander in the wilderness for 40 years?...He was a man, and he would not stop and ask for directions*, begs to be repeated and strongly suggests that the art of questioning comes more naturally to the female. Sorry, men.

Is it not obvious that we should ask directions from the One who journeys with us on life's musical path, personal path, professional path, and all other paths? Are we afraid that asking will be a bother? Are we afraid that, by asking, the Christ-King will somehow think less of us?

*Grace us with Yourself. In the name of our Mighty King we pray,*
AMEN.

# 39. Is Your Plate Full?

*Music deserves our attention. So does food. When music and food mix, on which one do you focus?*

The charitable Boaz allowed Ruth, who worked in his fields, to drink from animal skins filled with water and to eat bread soaked in vinegar.

*May the Lord reward you for your deeds, and may you have a full reward from the Lord, the God of Israel, under whose wings you have come for refuge!*
*~Ruth 2:12*

Why are we so busy all of the time? We do much of the busy-ness business to ourselves. We sign our kids up for things until they are big enough to sign themselves up for things. We volunteer. We work two jobs. We rise early and stay up late. We do the things that require doing, and we leave out those things that we would love to do. In a state of sheer exhaustion, we drag our bodies through the thresholds of our churches and fall into our assigned seats for choir practice. We sleep later on Sunday mornings and find it even more difficult to get up later after having had more sleep than we do on weekday workdays. We fall into those same seats for morning worship. Even the retired are so busy that they say, *We do not know how we had time to work all those years. In a way, life is as busy for us as it ever was.*

Is your plate full? Of course it is. In fact, if you are honest about it, you do not know many people whose plates are not just as full as yours is.[13] Nevertheless, you go to church, and you go to make some music in Jesus' name, and a magical thing happens. You leave the church building with a spring in your step. You find energy through the music and its impact upon your life. Listen as you exit your choir room. Someone will invariably say, *It was all I could do to get here tonight, but I'm glad I came. I have more energy now than I had when I arrived.* Music is a blessing for our lives. What an honor it is to make music at church.

*Brighten our souls with Your sunshine. In the name of the Bread of Life we pray,* AMEN.

# 40. What Color Stole Do We Wear?

*Music suggests certain moods and feelings. It is up to us as to whether we will actually go where the music is recommending we should go.*

When Paul counted loses, he counted things that he had actually lost, not the things that he might lose.

*More than that, I regard everything as loss because of the surpassing value of knowing Christ Jesus my Lord. For His sake, I have suffered the loss of all things, and I regard them as rubbish, in order that I may gain Christ.*
*~Philippians 3:8*

"Who 'stole' my stole?" the impish choir member asked. Scores of churches observe the liturgical year and use the colors that go along with such an observance. Choir people and ministers wear colors with their robes. The church year colors come in red, green, purple, white, and others too, depending on the tradition. It is always a big deal with these choirs that they a.) Wear the correct color that corresponds with the church calendar, and b.) Wear the same colored stole, at least, if the correct color chart eludes them before service time.

Often we will hear it said that someone has shown his or her true colors. A popular song from a couple of decades back declares, "I see your true colors shining through. Don't be afraid to let them show." This is good advice. As Christian musicians, we need to wear our bold colors boldly. We put on our robes, encircle our necks with splashes of color, and give witness to that which resides inside of us. Music flows out. We do not offer a fashion show or a concert. We offer more.

There are seasons in our souls that cry for color. Times of preparation and repentance –purple. For the holiest of occasions –white. Seasons of growth and renewal –green. The best color for representing the fire of motivation –red.

This is why a rainbow impresses us. When we see it, we see all of the colors of our lives at once and remember God's promises. Those promises renew each day. Now that alone is cause for song.

*Renew right spirits within. In the name of the Holy One we pray,*
AMEN.

# 41. When Is Easter This Year?

*Positive musical experience is the food that keeps musicians coming back for more.*

Because of Christ, we have escaped the bonds of sin and death. Our victory over these things is certain.

*But, I, with the voice of thanksgiving, will sacrifice to You. What I have vowed I will pay. Deliverance belongs to the Lord.*
*~Jonah 2:9*

We love to celebrate Christ's resurrection, but we do not like to dwell on the fact that His sacrifice on our behalf preceded it. Sometimes choirs grow tired of the sorrowful texts and tunes that serve as a prelude to Easter. They will voice their concern by asking the date of Easter, that highest and holiest of all days in the Christian calendar, that floating, egg hunting date that follows the lunar-solar calendar.

Easter, for the Christian musician, means that it is time to change life's melodic patterns in ways that express profound joy –not the hee-haw kind –but the profound joy of gratitude because of the eternal triumph of Jesus over sin; still, it is not only sin that He conquered --it is death as well. Easter is a thing for anticipation. The world waited so long for the Messiah, and then, as He appeared and began to change the world, His career derailed and His life ended miserably. All of the exhilaration seemed to be for naught.

Then the trumpets sounded.

CNN was not there, nor was any other representative of the media. However, on that morning, there had to be trumpets of angelic order. Imagine that the same celestial entourage that announced to herdsmen the birth of the divine babe were the same ones that blew the mighty blasts that heralded His emergence from the tomb of death. Those who sang, HE IS HERE now shouted HE IS STILL HERE!

Our Easter musical proclamations endorse that same message of a Jesus, born by miraculous means, who lived to perfection, and refused the sting of death. He won and made that same victory possible for all. Hallelujah!

*Shout salvation, full and free. In the name of our Salvation we pray,* AMEN.

# 42. Where Is That CD?

*You should like classical music. It sounds more like your life than you think.*

Saint and Peter are the first two words of oodles of jokes. Jesus gave him keys to His kingdom, true enough, but he was but one of the apostles who took Christ's message as far as he could to as many people as he could.

*I will give you the keys to the kingdom of heaven, and whatever you bind on earth will be bound in heaven, and whatever you loose on earth will be loosed in heaven.*
*~Matthew 16:19*

Music publishers create marvelous teaching aids for church music performance and accompaniment –compact discs, better known as CDs. Usually these have two takes, or versions, on them. The first has a demonstration of how the piece will sound when people are singing and instruments are playing. The second removes the vocal lines, leaving only the musical instruments to play the accompaniment. These CDs are expensive and well worth their cost, especially for those churches that actually use them to accompany their choirs during worship. It is very simple. Push *play*, and you have an instant orchestra at your command.

Singers love these recordings. It gives them a chance for extra practice anytime, anywhere. Those who feel less comfortable with their music reading or part learning skills use this resource to its fullest advantage. Confidence soars. Soloists have used these for a long time. All you need is a CD, a portable stereo player, and an audience. You are ready to perform. Bring on your nursing home ministry, your retreat ministry, or even your campground ministry.

But what if the CD gets lost? What if there is no electricity, no batteries, or no CD player? Now what are you going to do? You are going to do it the old-fashioned way. You are going to play the accompaniment on the piano or guitar or another accompanying instrument, or you are going to ask someone to play it for you. You are going to sing *a cappella*. You are going to manage without technology.

As wonderful as taped, or "canned" music is, it will never upstage authentic, live music. "Live" means "real," not "reel."

*Take us, and electrify our efforts. In the name of the Only Begotten Son we pray,* AMEN.

# VIII. Irreverent Questions

*Church musicians know no bounds. Their irreverent questions explore that which is off-limits or taboo. They challenge far more than conventional wisdom.*

*Jesus asked Irreverent (?) Questions:*

- *Why try this trick on me, you frauds? (Matthew)*
- *Why do you tempt me? (Mark)*
- *Is it lawful on Sabbath days to save life or destroy it? (Luke)*
- *Is it not written in your law, Ye are gods? (John)*

# 43. Do We Know That Hymn (Chorus)?

*Good music is but a taste of the heavenly concert that will one day be ours.*

Paul stood before King Agrippa, chained to one of his captors.

*Because you are especially familiar with all the customs and controversies of the Jews; therefore I beg of you to listen to me patiently.*
*~Acts 26:3*

The question at hand is massive in its appeal. Even those choir folk who rarely ask questions aloud move in to join this questioning. This inquiry appears to fit neatly into the conversation that follows. Singers get a facial expression that resembles the one used by those who use fancy vocabulary words properly in sentences. *Do we **know** that hymn?* Wait for it. Wait for it. (The expression... There it is.) It looks just like Barney Fife on those occasions when he shows great pleasure at the thought of being an authority on one thing or another.

You see, the person knows the answer before asking it. No, the hymn is not known, *unless Fred knows it, and, having grown up Lutheran in Nebraska, he knows a number of songs that we don't know.*

The inference is serious. *If we don't know it, we shouldn't sing it. If we don't know it, the congregation won't know it either. If it is foreign, it won't get a hearing. We don't know it, and we are not about to learn it.*

Even the most familiar songs were new at one time. Popular songs become popular as they move from obscure to well known as they play repeatedly over the airwaves. Mostly, worship planners do not select worship music material with fiendish chuckles. *We'll get them with this one, heh, hehheh, he he hehe.*

It is impossible to sing a new song with an old attitude.[14] It is not advisable to put new wine in old wineskins.

*Free us to desire holy changes. In the name of the Prince of Peace we pray, AMEN.*

# 44. Is the Piano in Tune?

*If you listen, you can hear the enormous amount of music
performed by nature's wind section.*

Any work begun by God will find completion according to
God's watch.

*I am confident of this, that the one who began a good work among
you will bring it to completion by the day of Jesus Christ.*
*~Philippians 1:6*

Remember, you can tune a piano, but you cannot *tuna fish*.
We should take these pithy words to heart. Some things are
tunable while others are not. When it comes to choral or
instrumental music, we find disparity. Singers spend little
time tuning in the instrumental sense. Yes, singers match
pitches played from a source, usually a piano, but singers
usually tune while they sing, adjusting chords along the way
in order to perfect them. Nobody does this as well or as
forcefully as the Barbershop quartet singers who live for
those moments when perfectly tuned chords ring out as
bands of steel from their throats.

Instrumentalists, on the other hand, spend tons of time
in front of intonation devices that tell them to pull or push
slides or other pieces of their instruments in order to
sharpen of flatten them to correct pitch. Instrumentalists, out
of necessity, are finicky about intonation.

When it comes to church instruments, like the piano and
organ, it is easy for churches to neglect their maintenance.
*How long since the piano had a tuning? I don't know. Who would
know? Did we have that technician over here last Christmas? I
think so. I could be mistaken.*

The churches who have switched from traditional
pianos to electronic keyboards do not have this concern. If
they have electricity, they have good intonation.

Congregations sing better when tuned instruments accompany them. People feel better about worship when instruments are in tune one with another.

All kinds of similarities could surface here about living lives tuned well to God's Word. That Word becomes the tuning instrument that we can fall on our faces in front of, and prayerfully ask God to give us tune-ups.

*Calibrate the ways we think and ways we do. In the name of the Cornerstone we pray, AMEN.*

# 45. Is the Organ Too Loud?

*Just imagine how many harmonica players there are in the world.
Aren't you glad they are not all in one place?*

Notice how the following reference from scripture has the
power of a poem, suggesting that members of the early
church could have easily sung this.

*Without any doubt, the mystery of our religion is great: He was
revealed in flesh, vindicated in spirit, seen by angels, proclaimed
among Gentiles, believed in throughout the world, taken up in
glory.*
*~1 Timothy 3:16*

Now we drop in on a telephone conversation between a
church organist and another person... We only hear what the
organist is saying...For the uninitiated, all of the terms used
here are organ terms. Very punny!

Organist: Great!
(Pause)
Organist: Swell!
(Pause)
Organist: Pedal harder, and wear the right Shoes!
(Pause)
Organist: It's the Principal of the thing.
(Pause)
Organist: How Rank is that!
(Pause)
Organist: What a Wind Chest.
(Pause)
Organist: Stop.
(Pause)
Organist: It's in the Manual manual.
(Pause)

Organist: Reed all about it.
(Pause)
Organist: How Consoling.
(Pause)
Organist: It's a Mixture.
(Pause)
Organist: Swell to Great.
(Pause)
Organist: That's a Pipe dream.

*Magnify Your power. In the name of the Lion of Judah we pray,*
AMEN.

# 46. Are We Listening to the Accompaniment?

*Look deeper. You will see music without even having to hear it.*

What goes around comes around.

*For the day of the Lord is near against all the nations. As you have done, it shall be done to you; your deeds shall return on your own head.*
*~Obadiah 1:15*

The accompanist is the choir person's best friend. The choir can sound no better than its accompanist can play. The accompanist can cover a multitude of choral mistakes or head off issues at the pass before they scream as sour notes customarily do. Some songs have those piano parts that are logical when compared to the vocal lines that are above them. Tons of choral literature feature organ parts that move as hymns move. The accompaniments of these make it easy for the singers to find their pitches and to burst forth in confident song.

Not all songs work that way. Some call on voices to do one musical idea while accompaniments provide contrast as opposed to continuity. Others mirror voices in coincidental time. When this happens, the music sounds like a conversation of sorts. It has give and take. It asks questions and gives replies between the inanimate piano and the animate human voice.

There are those songs that cause hearers to imagine that the singers are singing the accompaniment while the accompanist plays the true song. The most crucial thing is for the singers to listen to the accompaniment. It is there to dance along with them. Sometimes it leads, at other times it follows. By listening to the accompaniment, singers hold together by invisible, harmonic ties. There is spiritual oneness that distinguishes church musicians' work from those whose artistries seek after secular delights. The cacophony of life should find no place to resonate in the House of the Lord.

*Pray for us, O Lord. In the name of the King of Nations we pray,*
AMEN.

# 47. Where Did You Get This?

*The Beatles were once told that their sound was not what people wanted to hear and that guitar music was on the way out.*

David was a king on the run, fleeing his courts, taking his household with him and running from his own son, Absalom, who had found favor in the hearts of the people. David turned to one of his trusted servants:

*David said to him, "If you go on with me, you will be a burden to me."*
*~2 Samuel 15:33*

Not wanting to come right out and say how much he hated the song, the bass said to the director, after the first run through it, "Where did you get this piece of music?" The point struck like an arrow, and the message hit its mark. "So," the director said, "you don't like this one very much." "Not in the least," snorted the bass. "Too many runs, and it's way too high." "Remember the rule," the director said. "We do not pass judgment on a piece of music until we can sing it. Then, if we still don't like it...fine, we don't like it." For a second, the room was quiet. Then the bass gave his final verdict. "When we know it, it still will be too high, and it will have the same number of runs." Laughter enveloped the choir room.

Choir members usually do not suffer in silence. When they do not like their music, they usually give swift vocal opposition to it. Like most congregants, they nurture their opinions when it comes to music at their church. Only a few choir people love and live for the challenges that accompany musical tests that lie beyond the scope of a single rehearsal's mastery. Most prefer music that comforts rather than strains, reaffirms rather than causes concern.

Discerning choir people know that choirs should be ever stretching their repertoire and their musicianship. Just as church members would never wear the same outfits to church Sunday after Sunday and year after year, so should choirs be reaching beyond the singing of the same songs while, at the same time, never abandoning their favorites from days gone by.

What do you like about church music? What do you dislike about it? If you are honest, your answers will probably say a great deal about your faith.

*Work with our attitudes. In the name of the Man of Sorrows we pray, AMEN.*

# 48. Will You Sing Pianissimo, Please?

*Music frames silence..*

Our reliance must, out of necessity, rest on God, who alone
is faultless.

*All one's ways may be pure in one's own eyes, but the Lord weighs*
*the spirit.*
*~Proverbs 16:2*

Choirs love to sing loudly. It requires less thought and less
energy in a way. Singers want to skip down the path of least
resistance. This is the easy way for them.

One mezzo-soprano embodied this method of singing
when said she sang by *letter*. "I just open my mouth and *let*
*'er* fly."

"I like to sing *tenor* –ten or eleven blocks away, and you
can still hear me," said the male voice.

Then, of course, there are the timid songsters, like the
one who proudly told the visiting pastor, "I sing *solo* –so low
you can't hear me."

Most of life is neither soft nor loud. When you analyze it,
most days are average, and most songs, by volume, lay
toward the middle of the voice's dynamic capability. This is
the reason that we do not recall most of our days and save
the ones that are exceptionally wonderful and the ones that
are excruciatingly painful as the ones that we carry around
with us for a lifetime.

In music, performers can capture listener attention when
they play or sing energized, supported soft sounds.
Pianissimo. It makes the listeners listen more intently as they
pull near to the song. The whispers of sound scream for
attention. They usually get it.

In your music, be the kind of performer that observes
the dynamic indications. If you are always loud, people will

not listen to you. If you are always soft, your weightless decibels might contribute little to your group's overall effect. But...if you send your listeners to places that are as shifting as the surface of an ocean, then you are taking them to the places where the music is inviting them to be.

*Speak in accents clear. In the name of the Carpenter we pray,*
AMEN.

# IX. Hypothetical Questions

*Church musicians want to explore possibilities and test relationships. What would happen if......? Take a peek at some of their musings.*

<u>*Jesus asked Hypothetical Questions:*</u>

- *Why break God's commands because of tradition? (Matthew)*
- *What shall people give in exchange for their souls? (Mark)*
- *Shall God not avenge His own elect? (Luke)*
- *Do you love me more than anything or anyone else? (John)*

# 49.  Can We Get Some Air Conditioning?

*A great conductor once told the players as they were reaching for their instruments that they were already too loud.*

The following passage refers not only to Israel, but also to the Church triumphant:

*Then shall the young women rejoice in the dance, and the young men and the old shall be merry. I will turn their mourning into joy; I will comfort them, and give them gladness for sorrow.*
*~Jeremiah 31:13*

Church staff people know that it is impossible to please more than 80% of the people at any given time. If the skies were raining quarters, some people would be complaining about having to stack them. One person is too hot. The person sitting next to that person is too cold. This woman swoons from the aroma of others' colognes. That man gets a headache every time the florist brings in a Stargazer Lily. The cushions are too soft. The pews are too hard. Christians should be the happiest people anywhere, but so many times, they –we— are not.

Music people at church are no exception. The music is too high or low, too fast or slow. The music is too "high brow" or too Southern Gospel. The satisfied musicians sit quietly while the malcontented whine. Enough already!

For too long church music has been the whipping boy or the "War Department" for problems in the church. We do well to remember that music at church does not build a great church. It responds to one. Music people at church are just people who fail, squabble, disappoint, and fall short of God's holy plans. Perhaps church music draws criticism, not so much because of its susceptibility to discord, but because of its inherent visibility and audibility within church life. There is no place to hide musicians or their music. Church music people get an invisible report card each time they stand or sit before their congregations.

At church, people tend to be at their most sensitive selves, and in music, people tend to let their sensitivities shine forth. Put church and music together, and you have created an environment that has the potential for becoming highly combustible.

Get involved. Stay involved. Shake off thin skin. Cowboy up. The rewards are heavenly.

*Resolve our disputes. In the name of the Just One we pray,*
AMEN.

# 50. Did You Go to Sleep?

*Most people love the music they like while they detest the music they dislike. Duh!*

The seas of life get choppy at times. It is not advisable to sleep through a storm.

*The captain came and said to him, 'What are you doing sound asleep? Get up, call on your god! Perhaps the god will spare us a thought so that we do not perish.'*
*~Jonah 1:6*

It happens all the time. When some worshipers get still, they fall asleep. A few in particular are surfacing in your mind right now. No fair pointing... not even at yourself. There are the ones who simply close their eyes and drift off. The lips of some buzz gently and there are the ones who go into full-blown snore. A crowd favorite is the person who leans to one side or the other and catches consciousness just before falling out of the seat. Little children get a kick out of watching those too.

Most people do not go to sleep at church because they are bored. They go to sleep because church time is one of those rare times in the week when their bodies are not in motion. In the world of the overworked, underpaid, stressed out, burned out, overmedicated, and underappreciated, sitting down at church is a luxury.[15]

God could take church napping as a compliment and not an insult. The nappers find solace in the atmosphere of the redeemed. They take refuge in the arms of the Lord. They are safe, protected, and they embrace that security. They gain comfort by holy words and actions.

So before you give your next elbow to that person next to you in the House of the Lord, remember: Maybe the nap is the blessing they need. Maybe you should join them in slumber. Better still, maybe you should remain on guard just in case you need to grab them before they hit the floor.

*In the name of our Refuge and Strength,* AMEN.
*Awaken our lives for greater service, In the name of the Resurrection and Life,* AMEN.

# 51. Is It Vibrato?

*Some groups play sophisticated music...and lose.*

The Temple of the Lord is adorned as a bride preparing for her wedding.

*From their beautiful ornament, in which they took pride, they made their abominable images, their detestable things; therefore, I will make of it an unclean thing to them.*
*~Ezekiel 7:20*

Does your choir suffer from *too-much-vibrato-itis*? This is a common malady. Its cause is known. In the same way that, say, a violinist undulates the four strings of the violin in order to pull out all of the character and charm of a long note value, so do singers–but without a bow. Vibrato is actually a natural thing when the voice is free and its tone is produced without tension. A person singing alone does not have to match vibrato with any other person, so the rising and falling of the voice is not of gigantic concern...usually.

The trouble comes when a person plagued with ultra-vibrato begins to sing with others. It sounds much like an old truck trying to get started on winter's morn. WUH  wuh wuh  WUH WUH  wuh.

There is virtually no way to get this person's sound waves and crests in synchronization with those who sing along. It is always interesting to note how many famous opera singers are Italian. Their voices are magnificently adorned with vibrato. But how many great Italian choruses have you heard? Italian choirs tend to be choirs of soloists, and soloists have vibratos, and vibratos do not translate into good choral singing it would seem.

So, if your vibrato is wide enough to drive an 18 wheeler through and you sing in your church choir, you might consider speeding it up and narrowing it to make it more conforming to the other singers who share your songs. You really do not want to "stick out." It actually is not a compliment when someone from the congregation says, "I loved your song today. I heard your voice above all the others up there."

*Tame our voices. In the name of the Almighty, Which Is, Was, and Will Be, we pray, AMEN.*

# 52. May I Sit Next to Her?

*If you hang around great musicians, do not be surprised if you start to think and act as they do.*

God is the foundation of our hope.

*The Lord is good to those who wait for him,*
*to the soul that seeks him.*
*~Lamentations 3:25*

Sunday:

She said that she would join the choir if she could sit next to our very best singer. "She is classically trained," the new recruit said. "I need all the help I can get, so if you promise I can sit next to her, I will show up at the next practice. If not, the deal is off." The director waited for her to laugh or say that she was joking. She wasn't.

Thinking to himself that this was a very middle school-*ish* way of looking at church involvement, the director held his tongue and said something like, "O.K., come on," slightly under his breath.

Monday:

The director, replaying the conversation from the day before, laughed aloud as he was driving down the road. Ha! (in a high pitched, high maintenance voice like hers) "I'll join the choir if I can sit next to her."

Tuesday:

Running into the star singer at the grocery store, the director said, "You have real recruitment power. We are going to have a new choir member at this week's rehearsal. She said she would not join unless she could sit next to you."

"Who on earth would say a thing like that?" the celebrated choir member asked. "Why Lucille, that's who," the director responded as if reporting on the Six O' Clock News. "Lucille and I have together sung before," she snapped in response to the information. I do not wish to discuss this any further," she said before strolling on down the aisle to the fresh vegetables.

Wednesday:

(The director, in an email to the church secretary) Please contact all of the choir members and let them know that we will not have practice this evening. I'm really not feeling so well...

*Prepare us for those awkward moments. In the name of His Majesty we pray,* AMEN.

# 53. What Is a Descant?

*We are in this thing called life together. When it rains, we all get wet. When the sun shines, we all get to feel its warmth.*

Ignorance is no excuse from the law. When we know what our duty is, we need to do it.

*If you say, "Look, we did not know this" – does not he who weighs the heart perceive it? Does not he who keeps watch over your soul know it? And will he not repay all according to their deeds?*
*~Proverbs 24:12*

Consider Exhibit A –the descant. Listen as it floats above the choir. Observe its gentle, majestic leaps in directions contrary to the prevalent melodic line. To sing it, or not to sing it. That is the question. It takes rehearsal time to learn it. When learned it is a decoration. In no way is it necessary to the successful performance of the song. It is the whipped cream on top of the sundae. The dish is good without it, yet even more superior with it.

Sopranos are usually called on to sing descants. Tenors are no strangers to them either. *Say it isn't so. Des-cant be what we are supposed to be singing!*

Descants remind us that life has a prevalent tune to it, and as it moves along, there is almost an omnipresent din above it and a drone beneath it that might, or night not, contribute to its sustenance. It takes courage to step out of the comfort of melody to meet and greet the places where the descant is soaring. The descant is not the easy way out. *Let someone else sing it. Better yet, let someone play it. I'll stay where I am, doing what I have been doing, and getting the same results that I have come to know. They are not the most thrilling ones, but they are mine.*

Descants are anchored by their melodic foundations. They fly and usually return home. They know who they are.

They remember their origins. They want travelers to visit them with open eyes in order that they may see the landscapes they provide from a birds-eye perspective.

*Coach us to sing boldly. In the name of the Foundation we pray,*
AMEN.

## 54. Will the Organ Be Doubling Parts?

*The organ is such a fitting instrument for the church. Its power suggests God's power. Its variety of sound suggests God's variety of sound. Its complexity, made simple by skilled hands and feet, suggests God's complexity made simple by the Redeeming love of Christ.*

Some are entertained by your work. They admire your musical refinement, but they fail to feel the message that you support.

*To them you are like a singer of love songs, one who has a beautiful voice and plays well on an instrument; they hear what you say, but they will not do it.*
*~Ezekiel 33:32*

Sadly, numerous churches have organs but no one to play them. Finding an organist who is capable and willing to play for church services is rare. The necessary commitment level is heavy. Playing the organ is a rather solitary function, requiring hours of practice during times when all other church members are elsewhere. So, hats off to the organists who lend support to congregational song and spirit-filled praise.

Many choral pieces are written with accompaniments that read *for rehearsal only*, meaning the organ plays exactly what the choir sings in rehearsal and then drops out at the time of the actual singing. On those occasions, the organ, when it plays along, is actually another set of voices, augmented the work of the choral ensemble.

Some of the organist's work is lost to those who come to worship late. Some of the fruits of the organist's labor are lost by those who talk all the way through the final musical statement as they exit the worship. None is lost on the Lord for whom the music is a sacrifice of praise.

The mighty organ is the most powerful of all instruments. It is the king, just as the lion roars royally in the jungle. Its voice commands our respect. We hear it willingly. It speaks, through its various combinations of sound, to remind us of our diversity and our oneness in the Lord.

*In the name of the Offspring of David we pray,* AMEN.

# X. Sorting & Sifting Questions

*Church musicians allow questions to help them manage the acquisition of information. They are concerned with reliability.*

*Jesus asked Sorting & Sifting Questions:*

- *How many loaves do you have? (Matthew)*

- *What is your name? (Mark)*

- *Who can add one cubit to his/her height? (Luke)*

- *Where are your accusers? (John)*

# 55. Are They Out of Town?

*"Why are bagpipers always walking?" the critic asked. "They are attempting to get away from the sound," replied the jokester.*

As brothers, Jacob and Esau had made their peace. They did not travel together, as Esau had proposed, which was probably a good thing, given their personal differences.

*Then Esau said, 'Let us journey on our way, and I will go alongside you.'*
*~Genesis 33:12*

The Salvation Army knows something other Christian traditions have not caught on to as of yet. If you want to draw attention to your message, a good bass drum, a set of clashing cymbals, and a few wind instruments help immensely.

In church, we certainly know that Easter is more Easter-*ish* when a good trumpeter announces it. A church heritage emphasis, displaying a bagpiper, gets everyone all goose-fleshed. The clarinet, for some reason, makes a Hebrew-inspired tune all the more Jewish in tone.

Whenever bands play, they are apt to be on the move. There is a reason for this. They want to spread their sound to as many people as they can. Since it is impossible for crowds to get close to them, the band players take their shows on the road–to the people who want to hear them and enjoy their musical intensity.

Church music people are rarely together for the same rehearsal or the same service. It is as if churches have Group A, Group B, and so on. People get very excited when, on those rare occasions, all groups seem to be well represented at the same time. Let us remember that we have a musical witness wherever we are, wherever we go. That witness is not confined to our church and our choir. So, when you must be absent, try to find out where the parade lines are forming, and get in a good spot to experience the music that will inevitably come your way. Who knows? Maybe you can lend your gifts to those celebrations.

*Go with us when we go, for we need your company as we move through life's fertile and barren fields. In the name of the Lily of the Valley we pray, AMEN.*

# 56. Did She Not Do That At Her Other Church?

*Unfortunately, there are times when the only thing that hurts worse than people spreading lies about us, is when people spread the truth about us.*

The inner voice speaks to us. In the stillness of our days, when we find stillness, that voice is there to instruct as Spirit and as Truth.

*I do not understand my own actions. For I do not do what I want, but I do the very thing I hate.*
*~Romans 7:15*

Just as some children do not play well with others, some adults do not relate well with other adults. A few of these people join church choirs. The church music director who does not learn how to manage these ill-tempered souls and fails to diffuse their episodic ranting and raving will not enjoy a long, happy, or productive tenure among the people.[16]

Consider the church choir history of Rosa.

Rosa grew up in church and began singing solos at the age of 12. She was happy until the choir director at her rural congregation began asking other people to join in the solo rotation. Rosa was no longer the only "one." She packed her bags and left.

Rosa could sing. The problem was her feeling that she could do it better than anyone else. So, after about a year of not singing, she got her driver's license and began attending a larger church. They had "good music" there. They would understand her. She joined the choir. All was good... until one day she realized the director did not select music that was *cool* enough. She wanted to sing the songs she heard on televised church services. By this time, it was time for her to leave home for college. She would make a new start in a new church in her college's town.

There, Rosa was surrounded, for the first time, by those whose talents truly eclipsed her own. She began to speak ill of the abilities of others. She launched character assassinations on them all. She was miserable. People who had been her friends distanced themselves.

She stopped going to church. The people there were stupid and did not know what they were doing.

About 20 years later, she tried once more. By this time she had married, had children, and settled in a city some 300 miles from where she grew up. Rosa thought she would volunteer to direct a children's choir at the church around the corner from her home. It was not long before she wanted to change the structure of the established choirs. She wanted twice as many children to work with. Tempters flared. She quit.

She never went back.

*Break our destructive habits. In the name of our Redeemer we pray,* AMEN.

# 57. Do We Have Any Room?

*We do not have to understand music to be moved by it.*

Authentic meekness is part and parcel of wisdom.

*Who is wise and understanding among you? Show by your good life that your works are done with gentleness born of wisdom.*
*~James 3:13*

"_____ says he might be interested in joining the choir," the singer says to you, the director. You call him on the phone the next day. "_____ says you might be interested in joining the choir," you tell him. "That's why I'm phoning you now." "She did?" he replies. "I remember talking with her about some singing I did years ago in the church where I grew up," he continues, "but joining the choir? I don't recall saying that." "Well, I promised her I would get in touch with you," you add. "Do you have room for one more?" the would-be singer inquires. "I think we do. If you noticed, at our last service our entire back row was empty," you say with a wry smile. The encounter nears it conclusion with the candidate's words, "I suppose I could give it a try."

Church people sometimes act as if the choir area is a well-constrained piece of real estate, reserved only for a select few who hold free and clear titles to membership there. Like a reserved seat at a theater, only those who have the right ticket can sit in a certain section. In most cases, choir membership is for anyone who is willing to give it a try. To be certain, choir is not the best place of service for everyone, but blest is the person who gives it a trial run before saying, "This is not for me."

Who knows? Choir can be tried and found to fit like a glove with the lifestyles and church interests of the working professional, the retired, the stay at home, and the on-the-road-ers. Ask a choir person near you how it would feel not to identify with church choir. Ask them is they would even attend church if the choir disappeared.

*Join our gifts with Your plans. In the name of the King of Saints we pray,* AMEN.

# 58. Am I Late?

*Harpists do not get around to playing much music. They spend all of their practice time tuning.*

Do not be surprised that you wind up doing the things that the people around you are doing. We advise our children to watch the company they keep. So it is for most everyone.

*I urge you to put yourselves at the service of such people, and of everyone who works and toils with them.*
*~1 Corinthians 16:16*

Some people are late getting to church. These tend to be the people who are late getting to work, the people who are late getting to most all of their engagements. Why are they late? Let us count the reasons.

Well, there's...no, that wouldn't be a reason –that would be an excuse.

O.K., let's see...oh, we can't use that one either. It too falls into the category of excuse.

What about...that's more of a distraction than a reason, now that I think about it.

Hmmm.

Most church music rehearsals are in the evenings. Most people who participate in them work during the day. It is impossible for most of them to finish up at work, drive home, deal with after school events with children, conjure up dinner, and make it to rehearsals on time. Such people should be awarded medals when they arrive at church.

"But what if I'm late? Can I still be a part of things?" the choir person will ask the director. Depending on the circumstance, the answer is usually "yes."

God wants our praise. Offering that praise through music becomes a blessing to those who hear and especially to those who provide. The person who is out there moving heaven and earth to sing, play, ring, or direct at church is the person who knows the value of that sacrifice and cannot entertain the thought of giving it up, even when it means they will be late.

Directors take note: Do not move you rehearsal 15 minutes later to accommodate the straggler. That person will be late no matter when you practice.

*Order our steps in Your Word. In the name of the Counselor we pray,* AMEN.

# 59. Why Does She Talk During Rehearsal?

*Never get in the way of a person who is trying to make the music better.*
*The Lord loves our cheerfulness.*

What would we do for others if we had the opportunity to help them? Would we give them time? Money? Gifts? All of these things? Would we pray for them? With them? How would we determine their needs?

*For if the eagerness is there, the gift is acceptable according to what one has –not according to what one does not have.*
*~2 Corinthians 8:12*

It happens without fail. Every time we get to a place in rehearsal where the music must be thrashed, part by part, piece by piece, so that it can be just right, she starts to talk. Sometimes she blurts something out to the whole group. At other times she turns to the person adjacent to her and strikes up a conversation about the meal she prepared for her family or her aunt's husband's friend's brother, who is having some tests run next Monday at the medical center. Sometimes people talk back (which she loves), and the conversation is extended. Some times quick, polite comments are made hastily, and she settles down for a bit.

Why does she talk? There are several reasons. First, choir is a social event for her. To be sure, it has a social component as one of its benefits. Secondly, she loves to talk. Ever since grade school, her teachers and friends have pointed out this flaw. Next, she talks because she feels confident enough in the music to give it only a portion of her attention. In addition, her gift of gab spills over from her sincere desire to be friendly to her co-musicians. There is nothing inherently wrong with any of those reasons.

One of the frustrating things about a rehearsal for some people is that verbal directions are given for the benefit of the whole. If a person talks during these comments, the person misses it. Directions must be repeated. Time is wasted unnecessarily. Another problem with this is that a rehearsal is an everyone-doing-the-same-thing-at-the-same-time activity. The talker intrudes upon another person's participation in the work that is taking place. In the case of the church choir, the purpose has a holy implication, so the motives for doing the best job possible are strong.

Directors should give serious consideration to scheduling a way for people to say what is on their hearts during rehearsals so that the "talkers" can have their say without becoming white noise the rest of the time for the listeners.

*In the name of our listening God we pray,* AMEN.

# 60. Who Will Narrate?

*Give old "what's his name" the speaking part. That way we can get him out of the choir for that performance. Whew! Another problem solved.*

Jesus was doomed to death in order that we might find redemption.

*But now, says the Lord, He who created you, O Jacob, He who formed you, O Israel: Do not fear, for I have redeemed you; I have called you by name, you are mine.*
*~Isaiah 43:1*

Occasionally a choir will work on a piece of music that requires a speaking part. The speaking sometimes goes in front of the music, setting up the song. Mostly, narration takes place during an interlude of instrumental accompaniment. In either instance, the speaker must convey, through vocal inflection, the spirit of the text, just as the singers do when it is their turn to perform their musical parts.

When narrators talk over musical underscores, timing is crucial. Usually, composers have placed just enough time to get the prescribed words in before the next choral entrance. Any stumbling or losing place is surely met with problems. As in a dance, the talker does not want to step on the toes of the singers who are reluctant to sing when the speaker has more to say.

Numerous practice CDs exist and are marketed for the purpose of illustrating how easy it is to combine narrative passages with song. Each time the CD plays, perfection emanates from the electronic device. That man never trips over his tongue. That woman sounds like a radio announcer. This will be so easy for us to do. Ha. Ha. Ha.

Time for rehearsal comes. Take 1: The narrator is late making her entrance. We do it again. Take 2: The narrator enters with precision. All goes well until the choir makes its entrance a measure early. Take 3: Both narrator and choir count and everything is working according to the composer's plan. It worked. Everyone knows it did. Smiles permeate the rehearsal space. Now, to make sure we did not accidentally get it right, let us do it again. We do it again. The accompanist fails to observe the tenuto indication at measure seven. We stumble.

We go again.....

*In the name of the Lion of Judah we pray,* AMEN.

# XI. Inventive Questions

*Church musicians know that these questions turn our findings inside out and upside down.*

*Jesus asked Inventive Questions:*

- *May I not do what I like with that which belongs to me? (Matthew)*
- *Are you so without understanding? (Mark)*
- *If David called Him "Lord," then how is he His son? (Luke)*
- *Are these your words or the words of others? (John)*

# 61. Are the Handbells Playing?

*Music is a divine gift that ministers divinely.*

The garments of Old Testament priests had exact description in the second book of the Bible. Their priestly robes were adorned intricately and musically.

*They also made bells of pure gold, and put the bells between the pomegranates on the lower hem of the robe all round, between the pomegranates.*
*~Exodus 39:25*

It is rare to find a person who does not like handbells. You know handbells... those magnificently fashioned, foundry-produced instruments of tonal precision and beauty that add so much to times of worship. Perhaps your congregation does not have handbells, but you know what they are. You know what they look like and how they sound. Someone had the bright idea of taking the concept of church tower bells, the ones rung by pulling ropes, and bringing them down to earth so that people could not only hear them, but see them in all of their glory.

But there is an important distinction to make about handbells. Here it is: They do not make music. That is correct. Handbells are nothing but turned, tuned metals, expensively crafted for (almost) exclusive use in churches.

In and of themselves they just sit there on their lavishly padded tables. Oh, they look good, but they cannot say anything until willing hands clasp them, raise them, and swing them through time and space, revealing the auspicious sounds for which they are known and admired.

Seize the chance, if it ever avails itself to you, of ringing handbells. If your church is fortunate enough to have them, ask one of the bell ringers to show you how to, glove in hand, express yourself. You will be glad you did. Try to do it without smiling. I bet you can't.

Those bells call us to God, or, more accurately, it should be said that the personnel who set them in motion do.

*Enliven our spirits in ways that sparkle and shine. In the name of the Upholder we pray, AMEN.*

# 62. Can the Youth Do That?

*We tend to identify with the music that comes to us in our youth.*

Maybe you placed your trust in the Lord as a young person.
Maybe the Lord found you as an adult. Regardless of your
faith-walk, try to capture your world with child-like
innocence and youthful exuberance.

*Rejoice, young man, while you are young, and let your heart cheer
you in the days of your youth. Follow the inclination of your heart
and the desire of your eyes, but know that for all these things God
will bring you into judgment.*
*~Ecclesiastes 11:9*

When churches are fortunate to have vibrant youth groups
and capable youth leaders, music is somewhere in the mix.
Even if is not through choir *per se*, there is still music. Attend
youth functions and you will hear the strumming of guitars
(the youth group instrument of choice) and the singing of
faith choruses that bring cohesiveness to the group as a
whole.

In some churches, youth groups have their own times of
worship. In others, they provide regular service as featured
leaders. Most all churches have occasions when youth are
placed on a pedestal and/or provide worship leadership.
Smaller congregations allow for youth to be a part of their
church choirs, because there is no other choir for them to fit
into. Larger churches have youth choirs, some of which rival
small college choirs in terms of their superior musicianship
and quality of performance.

We need to acknowledge that teens are church leaders.
They are not the leaders of tomorrow; they are leaders of
today. They hold place and purpose in the Kingdom. Church
teens influence their peers in significant ways, and not on
their peers only, but on all who care deeply about their

development as people. They have voices and songs that need not be silenced by custom or schedule.

Let us not relegate youth music to retreat settings where congregations as a whole do not attend. Let us work to find opportunities to foster the musical development of teens who identify with our churches, and expect them to share their gifts during times of worship, study, and fellowship. Carve out experiences that allow them to teach and be taught. Strive to sing with them their new songs, and expect them to sing some old ones along with the adults who love them.

*Make me young enough to grow. In the name of the Lord of All we pray, AMEN.*

# 63. Does Anybody Play the Drums?

*Life has a beat to it. Sometimes we play along with recurring pulse.*
*At other times, we improvise around it.*

The beat is steady. The Lord is changeless. The beat is
continuous. The Lord reigns from generation to generation
and forevermore.

*Just and true are your ways, King of the nations!*
*~Revelation 15:3*

In this example, we check in with two neighboring church
choir leaders as they discuss percussion instruments in a
game of one-upmanship...

Leader A: Our choir did a piece last year that used
castanets.

Leader B: Oh, yeah? I know the song you are talking
about. We did it too, but we used claves and a guiro.

Leader A: I thought about doing that but the person
playing the castanets didn't have much room, you know,
with the timpani that we own over there in the corner.

Leader B: You guys have a timpani? Great. We enjoy our
set of *three*.

Leader A: Three? Wow. The person who plays ours is in
the local symphony.

Leader B: I was guest conductor of that symphony once.

Leader A: Does your Contemporary Worship feature a
full trap set? Ours does.

Leader B: Ours does too. The woman who plays it was a
band member of a guy who grew up in the same hometown
as the legendary Lionel Hampton.

Leader A: That's good. Say, if you ever need to borrow a
pair of congas, we have one.

Leader B: Thanks, but we usually just borrow ours from one of our members who owns a music store.

Leader A: Wow. Look at the time. I've got to be going. I am expecting our new Djembe (an drum of African origin Drum to be delivered.

Leader B: A Djembe? Are churches using those anymore?

*Put happiness into us. In the name of the Sent of the Father,*
AMEN.

# 64. Does the Score Include the Orchestra?

*Make your music, and, from time to time, give it an exclamation point!*

When Isaiah says "all nations," he issues a universal prophecy.

*He shall judge between many peoples, and shall arbitrate between strong nations far away; they shall beat their swords into ploughshares, and their spears into pruning-hooks; nation shall not lift up sword against nation, neither shall they learn war any more.*
*~Micah 4:3*

An orchestra is a beautiful thing. Look what it does to intensify a movie, such as *Gone With the Wind*. As the camera sweeps across the pastoral landscape of Tara Plantation during the film's opening credits, the orchestra swells to its fullest crescendo and fills in all of the gaps that Technicolor cannot paint.

Orchestral instruments, played in any combination, resonate with hues that traditional church keyboards, the piano, and even the organ, cannot match completely. Their introduction into churches is met with expectancy. When worshipers see instrumentalists ready to play, there is a strong signal that the church is about to do something for God, in a big way, and this is even before the players sound their first notes.

Not only do they spread aural colors, orchestras evoke wide ranges of emotions The orchestra can sound like a battle (Think of Tchaikovsky's *1812 Overture* –Ta, ta, ta, ta, ta, ta, taht, ta, taaah…BOOM, etc…). It can sound like a peaceful morning awakening to the dawn of a new day (Think of Copland's *Appalachian Spring* that features the beloved American Shaker tune, *Simple Gifts,* and that marvelous clarinet solo).

On occasion, even the smaller church that is not accustomed to live instrumental accompaniment will arrange for players to join with them for high/holy days and for special musical features sponsored by their churches. This provides joy and satisfaction to performers and listeners alike. Larger churches that produce regularly scheduled orchestral music in their church services should never take that blessing for granted, for theirs is a freedom of choice, flexibility, and variety that most churches do not understand. A solo instrument or ensemble adds life and zest. Nurture your instrumentalists as they provide music at church.

*Play Your music in our souls. In the name of the Ensign of the People we pray,* AMEN.

# 65. May We Take a Field Trip?

*How beautiful most all music would be if it were performed correctly.*

If you do not like the weather, wait awhile- it's bound to change. The seasons come and go, and so do your opportunities for Christian service. Take charge of your chances to make a difference in your church and in your community.

*For now the winter is past, the rain is over and gone.*
*~Song of Songs 2:11*

You know you are affiliated with a terrific church choir when you see its membership craving opportunities for social interaction. Admittedly, large choirs have grown beyond their ability to do family-type outings, but even in those cases, choir health can be observed in the several sub-groups that form from the group as a whole as they explore what it means to become "Church," one to another.[17]

The choir that needs help in this area would do well to consider these 12 ideas for socialization that reside outside of regular duties. There is a suggestion for each month of the year.

January: Hosting a blood drive through the Red Cross

February: Bringing your significant other to choir for a "sweetheart" rehearsal

March: Producing an "Irish" potato bar lunch after church with choir members' families

April: Sponsoring a community walk/run that can benefit a specific community charity

May: Visiting another church, different than your own, together

June: Traveling to a major or minor league baseball game and performing the National Anthem while there (?)

July: Attending the local fireworks show *en masse*

August: Finding a "sister" choir in another country

September: Holding a music ministry banquet/awards night

October: Going to a theatre performance, preferable a musical

November: Adopting a community family and providing a Thanksgiving meal for them

December: Caroling to nominated homes and nursing centers

In no way is this list intended to be an exhaustive. Let your imagination run wild. Have fun. Find meaning and value in what you do together.

*Take us to new spiritual places. In the name of the Everlasting Father, AMEN.*

# 66. When Do We Hear From the Children?

*The ones who appreciate your music are the ones who love you.*

Life is precious and God-given. We come into the world singing (in a manner of speaking). Thanks be to God!

*Just as you do not know how the breath comes to the bones in the mother's womb, so you do not know the work of God, who makes everything.*
*~Ecclesiastes 11:5*

The most wonderful thing happens when children sing at church. Everyone sits tall in the seats. Everyone pays close attention to the sounds of the performers. They smile. It is so easy to know who the children's parents are, and even easier to know who their grandparents are. So, the next time the children sing, if you can, try to look at the people, just for a little while, and not at the boys and girls. You will learn three things:

1. Nothing is more angelic to us on this earth than the sight and sound of children, who represent God's pinnacle of creation, unspoiled and full of hope for the future.
2. Nothing teaches us about God's love any more than babies who grow in trust and innocence and grow, physically, mentally, and emotionally, toward their maturity in life.
3. Nothing reminds us more of Jesus than these little ones. When most of us think of Jesus, we think of a man surrounded by boys and girls, and a man who delighted in their company.

Children are capable of such great music, for it springs from their hearts as pure joy. At church, they have it made. It does not matter how they sound. What matters is that they are there. That is what we hear –their presence among us.

Those who work with them in their songs know that they are eager to know more about Jesus and their work for His Kingdom and its advancement. Work diligently with them. Work quickly, before they get too "cool" to do it.

*Bring child-like wonder to our music. In the name of the Root of Jesse,* AMEN.

# XII. Telling Questions

*Church musicians use these questions to lead them right to the target of their concerns.*

<u>*Jesus asked Telling Questions:*</u>

- *What makes you lose your nerve? (Matthew)*
- *Why does this generation seek after a sign? (Mark)*
- *Did you go to the wilderness to see a reed shaken in the wind? (Luke)*
- *Why are you about to kill me? (John)*

# 67. Can We Bring in Some "Ringers"?

*Music can usher us into an awareness of God's presence. Its*
*vibrations cause us to celebrate and to wonder.*

We who love the Lord stand on the shoulders of the faithful
who have gone before us. We take our places in life and
death and seek to fulfill designations as redeemed saints.

*According to the grace of God given to me, like a skilled master*
*builder, I laid a foundation, and someone else is building on it.*
*Each builder must choose with care how to build on it.*
*~1 Corinthians 3:10*

From time to time, choirs have special services that are
called "Cantatas" or "Hymn Festivals" or "Song Services."
These times are full of musical emphasis, for the songs
comprise the sermonic material for such occasions.
Whenever this happens, someone invariably will say, "Can
we bring in some "ringers"? Ringers are those skilled
persons, available to choirs, who are so good that they can
come in, and with one rehearsal, make the sound of the choir
go up remarkably. Some "ringers" are former church
members, some are community members- friends from other
churches, and the like.

There are times when instrumental "ringers" are
required, because of ways in which the music has been
arranged. Often there are songs that would sound so much
more complete if they had the instruments called for in the
scores to accompany the singing. Securing "ringers" takes
time, and usually, a lot of money.

It is not uncommon for choirs to prepare material that
serves as a back up for a more prominent solo singer
("ringer") who has been imported for unique church music
concerts. Churches love hearing such talent, and choirs

appreciate the extra help in nailing down those difficult musical phrases.

The real work of the people is embodied by the people – those who are with the church week in and week out, through times of growth and times of decline –through seasons celebratory and sorrowful. The real church musicians are those who prepare and do their best during times that are ordinary. Some traditions even call it *Ordinary Time.*

"Ringers" have their place, but the regular cast of church musicians who sit to your right and left at most every practice and praise (and you included) are the real stars.

*Make the ordinary--extraordinary. In the name of the Word Made Flesh we pray,* AMEN.

# 68. Did They Like It?

*It is not all exciting. It is not all inspiring.*

Nahum warned the people about leaders who are careless and possess false senses of security.

*Your shepherds are asleep, O king of Assyria; your nobles slumber. Your people are scattered on the mountains with no one to gather them.*
*~Nahum 3:18*

When a person sings or plays at church, there is always that inward question that infiltrates the mind, "Did they like it?" ("they" being the worshippers)... Notice that the question is not, "Did they like me?" The real church musician is beyond all of that business and knows that it is the message, not the messenger that is the important thing at church. The message will always be greater, and this is what God deserves and desires.

Church musicians must know their audiences. What will be liked in this church will not be appreciated in that church. These styles of music are accepted in this part of town while that set of styles is not. Many times the style of the music, its overall sound, or its instrumentation, will determine how it is received, no matter how well or how poorly it is performed.

Take, for instance, the choir that sings a flawless *a cappella* rendition of Tomas Luis de Victoria's "O Magnum Mysterium" and the choir that sings an error free run of Mary Mary's "Shackles (Wanna Praise You)." Both choirs have done a superb job and are well received by their listeners in their home congregations. Now, exchange the choirs for next Sunday's services, let them do just as well as they did on the previous Sunday, and watch as they go over like lead balloons with the congregations.

It takes an open mind to accept a message, musical or otherwise. Offense is given, even when it is not intended, when a message is packaged as a gift that is dismissed even before it is unwrapped.

If your work is preoccupied by the stress of worrying about is acceptance, then just how on earth are you going to be happy or true to yourself?[18]

*Save us from ourselves. In the name of our Spiritual Rock we pray,*
AMEN.

# 69. Do We Have to Be Here?

*What if there is no one to hear you?*

It does not matter how many people are in your church music group. It does not matter how many people hear your weekly efforts at praise. What matters is that you are aware that your work returns to the ear of the Lord.

*I declare what I have seen in the Father's presence; as for you, you should do what you have heard from the Father.*
*~John 8:38*

Church buildings ought to be full of life. Healthy churches have meetings, events, rehearsals, services, and fellowships going all the time. Special gatekeepers such as secretaries are charged with juggling all of this so that more than one group does not show up at the same time in the same space. Many congregations sponsor community groups that use church facilities, and this is on top of in-house church functions.

At rehearsals, choir directors announce, through spoken or written words, how choir duties relate to other ministries that are going on in churches.

Church is not just for choir people –Oh? The work of church music is but one piece of the pie, one banana of the bunch.

Frequently, music is called for at non-music/worship gatherings. Sometimes it is not. When forecasts are made about the various activities of church life, choir members want to know if they "have to attend." What they mean is, "Will we be presenting music for whatever is going to be happening?"

As silly as it sounds, most church people feel the need to be invited to things that occur in their churches. This is a normal and natural reaction to the telling processes that go on in real life. For music people, it is a snap to know how to fit in and find a sense of place at church. For numerous others, it is more of a trial and error kind of thing. In churches with multiple ministries, seekers can experiment with this and that until they find their niche.

Musical ladies and gentlemen find it improbable that they should attend church as civilians –those who face the pastor as opposed to always looking at his or her backside or profile or from the lofty height of a balcony.

*Sit with us and remain. In the name of the Son of the Living God we pray, AMEN.*

# 70. Is This For Sunday?

*Words alone allow us the privilege of repeating them at will until we grasp them. Music flows along, uninterested in stopping and starting, and is all about its progression.*

Ready! God wants us to be prepared to follow God's ways. Set! God wants us to set our purposes in order that we might pursue God's precepts. Go! God wants us to go into God's world without being consumed by it.

*I pray that the sharing of your faith may become effective when you perceive all the good that we may do for Christ.*
*~Philemon 1:6*

"Is this for Sunday" is the #1 most commonly asked question by church music people. Here are some of the ways they sling it around:

1.  The choir has completed, rather successfully, an anthem during a routine mid-week rehearsal. *Is this for Sunday?* the tenor on the third row, second from the end on the director's right asks. This is the *I hope so-Is This For Sunday.*
2.  The choir, struggling with the contrast section, pages 4-5, of a particular piece. After several tries, a few, but not all of the parts have learned their correct pitches. *Is this for Sunday?* asks the petite alto who sits close enough to the director's music stand that she fears she will be struck by the choral baton when it is used. This is the- *Our director is crazy if she/he thinks this can be ready for Sunday- Is This For Sunday.*
3.  A choir member who has been absent three of the past four choir practices holds up a piece of music from her soprano folder, waves it at the choir leader, and asks the one-breath double question, *Have we*

*sung this yet? Or Is this for Sunday?* This is the –*I really do not know what is going on around here*- Is This For Sunday.

4.  The two basses, as if intended in perfect unison, simultaneously hear a song called to rehearse, and they realize that they do not have a copy of it. *If this is for Sunday, I don't have it,* they say as one voice. This is the *We always seem to run out of music before it gets to the back row* –Is This For Sunday.

*Show us that our musical offerings are for Sundays and for every day. In the name of the God of Hosts we pray,* AMEN.

# 71. Where is My Music Folder?

*Music is a gift that you can give and receive. Give some. Get some.*

You become a gift to others when you volunteer your talents for the Lord. Your labor is a natural reaction to the grace that has been given freely to you and received freely by you.

*I, Paul, write this greeting with my own hand. This is the mark in every letter of mine. It is the way I write.*
*~2 Thessalonians 3:17*

One of the prime locations for outright theft is in a choir room. Either that, or little fairies descend on choral folders and pull music out when no one is around so that the next time the folder is opened there will be nothing there except for the music that has already been used in worship and should have been turned in to the choir librarian two weeks ago. If you sing in a choir, or if you used to sing in one, you are familiar with the question, "Where is my music"?

Soprano: Where is my music? It's missing.
Alto: Where is my music? I put it right here, and now it's gone.
Tenor: Where is *my* music?
(It's starts to sound like a rendition of Goldilocks and the Three Bears...*Someone's been eating my porridge, and it's all gone!*)
Bass: I don't have any music in here. I need everything.
Soprano: Me too.
Alto: Me three.
Tenor: I need a copy of the song for next week. Oh, wait, I have three copies of it in here. How did I wind up with three copies?
Soprano with bifocals: I can't share, so don't ask me to.

Alto with trifocals: If I don't get my own copy, I will have to go back home.

Director: The people who are not here all have copies of this. It appears that they have taken their folders home with them. So, not only are they not here, but their copies of the music aren't either.

Choir in Unison: Buy more copies next time.

*Grant us the resources we need. In the name of the Messiah we pray, AMEN.*

# 72. When Is Rehearsal?

*I am glad to invest my life in music. I do not recall meeting anyone who has said, "I wish I didn't read music," or "My life would be happier if I could remove all music from it." Like it or not, music wants to befriend.*

We will never be worthy of the favor that we know from on high, so we, even more, should desire to be eager in our acts of service.

*At that time gifts will be brought to the Lord of hosts from a people tall and smooth, from a people feared near and far, a nation mighty and conquering, whose land the rivers divide, to Mount Zion, the place of the name of the Lord of hosts.*
*~Isaiah 18:7*

"When we don't have choir rehearsal, I really miss it," the alto said. "I know, right? When we don't practice during those last few weeks of summer, I get my days turned around," the other alto agreed.

For church musicians, choir becomes engrained in our rhythmic responses to life. It helps to define us. There are those for whom choir rehearsal is about their only outlet, their only break from the have-tos and the must-dos that come with the numerous hats they wear. Choir contains those essential vitamins and minerals that are essential to a healthy Christian life, so the absence of choir rehearsals, especially the absence of several in a row, begins to take its toll. There is an obvious loss, something akin to an iron deficiency that grabs hold of the singers when this happens.

Many of the biblical passages we know from memory are because we know songs that contain them. Most of the systemic, theological frames that we call our faith are manufactured by words that are scored into our brains by our associations with songs, hymns, and spiritual songs.

Most of the terms that we use to describe our feelings about the life of a Christian come from the faith songs we know best and the ones we hear on Christian radio, or on the ubiquitous Christian CDs that we play in our cars as we travel.

Habit forming choir membership is good for mind, body, and soul. Give your mind to it by cheerfully blending your talent with those talents of everyone else. Give your body to it by being present whenever something is going on. Give your soul to it by praying for your musical leadership and your Christian friends that you find at your church.

*Occupy our days with the music of the redeemed. In the name of Christ we pray, AMEN.*

# XIII. Clarification Questions

*Church musicians who ask these questions turn fog and smog into meaning. How did we get to this point? Clarifying questions try to find out.*

<u>Jesus asked Clarification Questions:</u>

- *Do not babes and infants give perfect praise? (Matthew)*
- *Whose image is on this coin? (Mark)*
- *Why are you troubled? (Luke)*
- *Why do you ask Me such things? (John)*

# 73. Am I Singing the Right Note?

*There is a simple formula for great musical interpretation. All you have to do is get everything just right.*

Usually, we do not like it when someone corrects us. God, through prophetic preachers, scolded Israel for her wickedness and superstitions.

*It has listened to no voice; it has accepted no correction. It has not trusted in the Lord; it has not drawn near to its God.*
*~Zephaniah 3:2*

One of the things that singers are most sensitive about is pitch, so singing the correct note is of paramount importance. No singer wants to clash with others in an amusement park-like ride of aural bumper cars. The result of a wrong note produces a sour moment that dulls the beauty of the song and robs the singer of needed confidence.

That is the way it is with the living out of our faith also. We want to get it right. We do not desire to stick out in a bad way. We do not want to call negative attention to ourselves. For one thing, that would produce awkward moments. For another thing, it would mean that we are lacking in one form or another when it comes to Christian maturity.

Maybe it is O.K. to miss a note now and again. Maybe when we do we should really, really miss it with a loud and off-beat yawp that leaves no doubt as to the offense or its perpetrator. Maybe then, and only then, can we begin to grow as music makers, leaning not on the stronger, more successful ones around us to pull us through, but on our own gifts and ourselves. I hope that we are changing, and for the better, every day.

It is going to take some work, this business of getting all of the notes right. There are no money back guarantees on performing right notes, and past performances of them do not predict future results in a definitive way. We just have to keep plugging along.

*Help us to reproduce what composers intend, and help us to sound that intent with gusto. We make this prayer in the name of the Author and Finisher of Our Faith. AMEN.*

# 74. Are We Under the Pitch?

*Once upon a time, you could carry a tune in a bucket, but now your bucket has a hole in it.*

We are fed by the earth. We harvest food from its land and sea. When we are not good stewards of our natural resources, we are ungrateful to God for our harvests.

*As for the earth, out of it comes bread; but underneath it is turned up as by fire.*
*~Job 28:5*

It is so easy to sing out of tune. And when it happens, the ear is not pleased. We know about breath support, lifting the soft palate, having tall vowels, and all of the other things that singers can do to help ensure tonal accuracy. However, sometimes, when a pitch stays too high for too long or we are asked to sing sustained, descending half steps, what we know and what we produce can be two different things.

We listen to others. We hear those for whom intonation appears to hold no challenge. We hear others who, try as they might, never seem to match a true pitch no matter how many times they sing the same song. They get to difficult passages, and you know what is coming. It causes you to turn your head sideways and in an upward direction in hopes that your craned neck will sharpen their pitch. Most of the time, they do not know what you are doing or why you are doing it. How challenging it is to be in the vicinity of those who, in off-key mode, flippantly move through a musical line, completely oblivious to the error of their vocal ways.

*When in doubt, do not sing out,* you want to shout at them, but it would do no good, for they are blissfully unconcerned about their lack of precision.

It is like this as we live our lives. What we know and what we do are often not reconciled. How can others see things in us that we dare not see in ourselves? Maybe because it is much easier to vocalize than it is to analyze.

*Be for us a looking glass. In the name of our Strong Tower we pray,* AMEN.

# 75. Can We Go Over That Part Again?

*Practice. Practice. Practice. Repeat.*

There are those times when what we say and mean do not add up. Similarly, our music jumbles when we fail to interpret the mood as well as the message of a song.

*As we have said before, so now I repeat, if anyone proclaims to you a gospel contrary to what you received, let that one be accursed!*
*~Galatians 1:9*

When you have sung for a while, you learn how to scan a piece of music quickly, looking for any potential tough spots. You know where they are even before you hear the piece for the first time. These are the places that have the highest tessitura, the biggest leaps, the accidentals. You know that when you get to those places in the song, you are going to have some potential issues about getting things to come out right.

In rehearsals, directors often isolate those musical sections that are the most demanding. Why spend precious rehearsal time plowing through the places that choristers have down pat? It is judicious to deal with the problems before they become engrained through mindless repetition without correction.

So, when a music leader asks, "Can we go over that part again?" it is a very polite way of saying, "We really *need* to go over that part again."

Life, like a music rehearsal, requires work. Some music participants are eager to join church choirs until they discover that those choirs have to work so long and hard to achieve beneficial results.

How satisfying it is to work through life's problems a step at a time, just as we do in our purposeful music rehearsals, with music that does not readily fall in place. If choir affiliation teaches us nothing else, let us not be reluctant to acknowledge its connection to real life and our need to rely on God's grace and unfailing love to guide us through those trials that will surely come our way.

Learning music is not the end of it all. Learning about our relationship with God is.

*Repeat the sounding joy. In the name of the Builder we pray,*
AMEN.

# 76. How Many Stanzas Will We Sing?

*The Bible is the Word of God. When it is read, it wants to be read
completely. All of its verses call for the reader's attention.*

We are God's work. God wants to work in us.

*O Lord, I have heard of your renown, and I stand in awe, O Lord,
of your work. In our own time revive it; in our
own time make it known; in wrath may you remember mercy.*
*~Habakkuk 3:2*

It has been said that, in most churches, you would not want
to be a front pew in a sanctuary or the third stanza of a
hymn. If you are that seat or that stanza, you are rarely sat in
and rarely sung.

Standard performance practice in many churches is to
introduce a congregational song in a certain manner. For
example, the hymn, chorus, *whatever*, is played through, in
its entirety, before the singing begins. Or, there might be a
certain way that hymns are sung. Again, for example, the
choir sings unison on all first and last stanzas, and sings all
written choral parts as written on all middle stanzas.

Another common understanding is that a complete song
will not be sung, when singing from the church songbook.
Commonly, a music leader in such a church will announce
the song to be sung and to say something like, "We will be
singing the first, fourth, and fifth stanzas only."

How would the poet who wrote the song feel about the
omission of a complete segment of the original poem? Why
is the stanza being left out? To save time? To keep people
from singing too much? As long as you have a reason other
than *that's just what we do here*, everything is probably
alright.

Maybe that third stanza is the very one that expresses
the true meaning of the hymn the best. Maybe that third

stanza brings a continuity of thought to the hymn that is sorely lacking when it is omitted.

We want to taste all that God has in store for us. We do not want to leave anything out.

*Lavish heaping portions of blessings upon us, O Lord. In the name of the Righteous Judge we pray, AMEN.*

# 77. Will It Work If I Sing It With You?

*If you really listen, you will hear music in poetry. Even the most insensitive among us should feel the rhythm of words.*

Help someone, because Christ cares for you and sends others to comfort you. Give, not to receive, but know that through your giving you will receive.

*If he has wronged you in any way, or owes you anything, charge that to my account.*
*~Philemon 1:18*

Let's listen in on an after church parking lot conversation between a member of the choir and the music director...

**Choir Member:** We missed all of page 5 today. Did you hear how bad it was?

**Music Director:** I knew you guys were having some problems, but it didn't sound all *that* bad.

**Choir Member:** Why don't you ever sing with us? If you had helped us out today, we would have gotten back on track.

**Music Director:** Well, you know, directors are not supposed to sing all that much with their choirs.

**Choir Member:** Who said?

**Music Director:** That's what they teach us in choir director school.

**Choir Member:** That's the silliest thing I've ever heard of.

**Music Director:** There's the academic world and the real world...

**Choir Member:** We need you in the real world to sing with us when we hit the white caps.

**Music Director:** Count on me, but when I sing I'll do my best to blend in with the choir.

**Choir Member:** Thanks. I know what you mean. We had a music director here once who was like Gladys Knight, and we were the Pips.

**Music Director:** See... We don't want to go back to that.

**Choir Member:** We wouldn't need you to sing at all if our people came to church as they should.

**Music Director:** Our average attendance is about half of our singers on any given Sunday.

**Choir Member:** Have a good week.

**Music Director:** You too. **(Choir Member drives away) Music Director (aloud but to himself):** Just Call Me "Gladys."

*In the name of Jehovah we pray,* AMEN.

# 78. Who Sings the Middle Part?

*The middle is not the foundation. The middle is not the melody.*
*The middle is...uh...in between the two. That's why they call it the*
*middle.*

The tree in the first garden was off limits, not because of a
poisonous quality of fruit, but because it served as a
boundary, separating God from woman and man.

*But God said "You shall not eat of the fruit of the tree that is in the*
*middle of the garden, nor shall you touch it, or you shall die."*
*~Genesis 3:3*

"O.K. Let's stop and regroup," the director said. "As you
see, the women split into three part harmony at Rehearsal
Letter B. Let's see a show of hands. Who usually takes the
middle part?" Several hands will go up. Ironically, the
women who do not like to sing higher notes will not move a
muscle. "Why are you not volunteering for those notes,
Mildred?" Mildred shrugs her shoulders. "How about you,
Alma?" Alma laughs. "I'd rather stay with the melody," she
says.

The middle part is the hardest for singers to hear. It
demands the utmost in concentration. It colors the chords of
the ensemble. Those who sing middle parts do not
appreciate the designation Soprano II, for it denotes a kind
of second class something that knocks off a bit of the joy that
comes with singing it well.

When the men try to make the same vocal detours like
middle part-singing, they react in much the same ways. It
usually takes a music reader to make it work. In any event,
the singer, male or female, has to use the services of good
musical ears for proper intonation and balance.

Politically, the middle ground appears to be the safest
path to attract voters. Musically, the middle path is the most

tedious to navigate.[19] Choir directors need to recruit more middle people. More people need to aspire to be middle people. They really do come in handy when the going gets tough with the music. On second thought, maybe directors should stop purchasing music that divides in those ways. Just kidding. If they did, we would miss out on some beautiful sounds that highlight words of holiness.

*In the name of Jesus we pray,* AMEN.

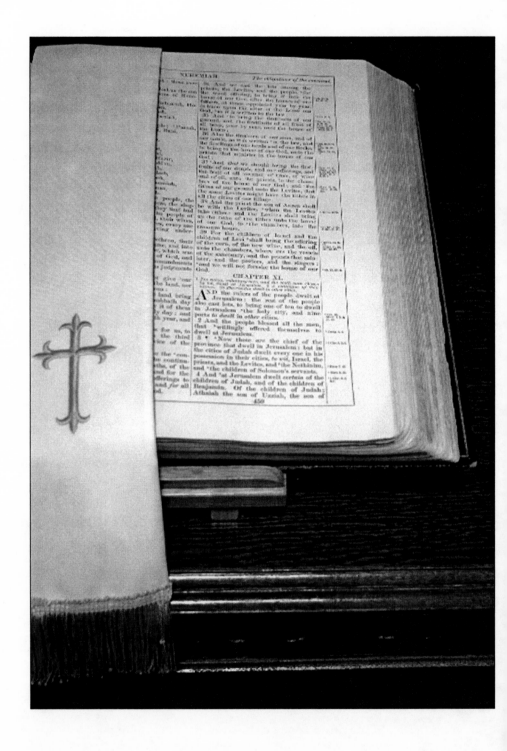

# XIV. Provocative Questions

*Church musicians use these questions to push, to challenge, and to throw conventional wisdom off balance. Provocative questions give free reign to doubt, disbelief, and skepticism.*

<u>*Jesus asked Provocative Questions:*</u>

- *Are you jealous because I am generous? (Matthew)*
- *Faithless generation, how long will I be with you? (Mark)*
- *Can the blind lead the blind? (Luke)*
- *Did I not say that if you believe you will see God's glory? (John)*

# 79.  Can I Sing Since I Cannot Practice?

*Those of us who feel the gentle tug of music in our lives are hard-pressed to imagine life apart from its beauty and its insistence that we follow it.*

Music, presented to the Lord, poses powerful occasions for deciphering what the Holy Spirit wants us to know, to be, and to do. Be open to the messages that are meant for you.

*The Lord rewarded me according to my righteousness; according to the cleanness of my hands he recompensed me.*
*~2 Samuel 22:21*

"I can sing on Sundays, but my work schedule will not allow me to come to rehearsals." Once spoken to the church choir director, a moment of decision has come. If the singer is told that attending choir practice is a must in order to sing on Sundays, the director is viewed as one who is dictatorial. If the singer is told to come on anyway, those who move heaven and earth to attend rehearsals are as upset as the proverbial laborers in the vineyard (see Matthew 20) who worked all day in the heat of the day, only to receive the same wages as those who worked for only an hour at the setting of the sun.

Obviously, it is not the intent of these brief statements to solve this dilemma; however, some guidance can be offered for developing a policy, like Rotary International's Four-Way Test, that provides truth, fairness, goodwill, and benefit for all.

Some church music leaders answer this way: "When you can put a Wednesday rehearsal and a Sunday service back-to-back, come on over and join us." Some will say, "You know, we warm-up 30 minutes before each service. Could you make that in lieu of rehearsals?" Some leaders will poll the choir for assistance in policy-making. At all cost, avoid the *soloist-mentality* that is embodied by those who can always find time to sing alone but who can never find time to sing with a group.

Desire has much to do with this. The person who is called into service will find ways to fulfill that call. It just always, always seems to work out that way at church.

*Teach us to number our days, that we may apply our hearts unto wisdom. In the name of our Refuge From the Storm we pray,*
AMEN.

# 80. Can We Get a Projector?

*Music is not, in and of itself, miraculous, but many of us allow it to transport us to miraculous places where our emotions are salved and our spirits find release.*

As communicators, we have come a long way. Let us never forget, though, the power of the personal telephone call or the hand-written letter or the real book-in-hand.

*Then afterwards I will pour out my spirit on all flesh; your sons and your daughters shall prophesy, your old men shall dream dreams, and your young men shall see visions.*
*~Joel 2:28*

If you will, remember a time when cell phones, personal computers, fax machines, and iPods did not exist. If you are too young to do that, just keep reading anyway. If you do remember a time when these things did not exist, it may be possible that you have been resistant to some of the changes that have come down the pike through the great and evolving renaissance that is technology. Most churches are reactive as opposed to proactive when it comes to technological advance. Is it permissible with you to use the word "technological" and immediately follow it with the word "advance"? Are wires and circuits tools for worship?

Choirs all over our great land are using technology to assist them in leading congregations in worship.[20] This is most commonly done by projecting words and images on church walls (yes, the writing *is* on the wall, so stay alert). Many times these words are visible to both the people in the pews and to the choir people as well. Do you have to have this kind of technology to have church? Of course not. Is it a viable means of communicating *Good News?* Of course it is.

Caution: Technology, just like music, must be rehearsed in order to bring it to its fullest effect. So people who run sound boards, lighting panels, and computers in worship should rehearse their parts with the seriousness of the musicians whose ranks they have now entered as *ex-officio* members.

Technology must add, not detract. Technology is not the message. It is a means to communicate the message. The early church did not depend on wireless microphones or PowerPoint presentations to preach the saving message of Jesus Christ. Neither should we. If you are riding the wave, good. If not, do not suspend your efforts on behalf of the Lord until your synthesizer arrives.

*Speak to us a common word in many voices. In the name of the Light of the World we pray,* AMEN.

# 81. Do You Need a Microphone?

*Take a day, and observe all the things that do and do not exist in harmony. Then take a day and do the same exercise using people as your gauge. You will be amazed at the consonances and dissonances that surround you.*

The Children of Israel prepared to observe the Feast of Tabernacles, an autumn festival that lasts for seven days.

*And that they should publish and proclaim in all their towns and in Jerusalem as follows, 'Go out to the hills and bring branches of olive, wild olive, myrtle, palm, and other leafy trees to make booths, as it is written.*
*~Nehemiah 8:15*

Voice teachers will tell you that you do not (should not) need a microphone if you are singing correctly.

Directors will sometimes say the same thing.

Directors will sometimes say that you *have* to use a hand-held, or a lavaliere, or a standard microphone when you are singing as a soloist or an ensemble member.

Even more widespread are the omni-directional microphones that suspend above choirs, picking up sounds from wide areas in order to project choral sound toward congregations. These are endorsed by most all directors – they love the sound boost, and they enjoy the fact that these mics are more invisible.

A microphone does not make a bad singer a good one, neither does it make a proficient singer sound terrible. It is what it is. A microphone is a tool that helps to deliver a message. Pastors use mics for the same reason.

Microphones do not make music, but they want more respect from musicians. Every day across the land they are struck on or about their heads by those who ask, *Is this thing on?* And then, immediately thereafter follow up with, *Whoa, can we get this thing turned down a little? I'm afraid we'll get feedback* (Feedback is a microphone's way of telling you that it is displeased.). Be nicer to mics. They haven't done anything to you.

Mics do not make you urbane. They have no curative powers. Do not use them unless you have to. Of course there are many times when you have to. When you have to, remember, you cannot hold them too close, but you can hold them too far away. When you use them, do not be shy. They like to be kissed.

*Empower Your message that we gladly proclaim. In the name of the Great Power we pray, AMEN.*

# 82. Is That in the Bulletin?

*Just as our spoken words have inflection- rise and fall- so do our notes. Rarely do we say or play the same things the same way twice.*

It is an admirable trait to tell the truth in love. It is a remarkable skill to walk the truth you speak.

*I was overjoyed when some of the friends arrived and testified to your faithfulness to the truth, namely, how you walk in the truth.*
*~3 John 1:3*

Church Musician (traditional church):
Heaven help us. If it's not in the bulletin, we don't do it.
Church Musician (contemporary church):
Bulletin? What is a bulletin?
Church Musician (liturgical church):
We do not prescribe the order of service; it prescribes us.
Church Musician (mega church):
People don't want bulletins. People want books.
Church Musician (emergent church):
A bulletin is nice, but people love the intrigue of not having one. So, not having one is nice too.
Church Musician (seeker church):
A bulletin might scare off those who lack background in church.

Continue, oh you churches, with your careful planning...with your spontaneous bursts of song. Continue with your precise executions of things rehearsed and your improvisational exercises in creative discernment. Stay the course of following the church year. Stay current. Remain inclusive. Stand for something so you will not fall for anything. Be predictable and keep them guessing. Love the Lord your God. Sing for Him. Play for Him.

Reach in and out for Him. Listen to the distinct rhythms of your heart...His heart. Bind yourself to Him, leaning not on your own understanding. Do not allow anything or anyone to tell you that we all have to be alike to see Jesus, or that once we see Him, we will become alike, or have the same interests or approaches to service in His name.

Love the people who surround your religious voice. If you have a bulletin, write inside of it the names of your many songs of worship. On its cover, write boldly these words: We take our mandate for Christ Himself, who commands us to do three things: Love the people, Love the people, and Love the people.

*Enlarge our vision. In the name of the Everlasting Father we pray,*
AMEN.

# 83. May We Sing Something We Know?

*There is music out there that you do not like. Remember, music does not feel as you do, so your distaste does not affect it. On the other hand, performers are a different lot. Tell them that you do not like their music –well, that is another story.*

Most of us have those favorite slippers that fit so perfectly on our feet or those woolen pajamas that warm us on wintry evenings. Many of us have those foods that soothe our spirits when the world has been cruel and demanding. So, too, are certain songs that speak to us when and where we need to have a palliative applied to our souls.

*Then Jacob awoke from his sleep and said, 'Surely the Lord is in this place –and I did not know it.*
*~Genesis 28:16*

Typically, the plea comes from members of the congregation. "May we sing something we know for a change? We're always asked to sing some obscure song that we have never seen or heard before, and *you* expect us to like it. Let's, at the very least, sing one thing in every service that people know by heart." There are times when choir members pick up the refrain, "Let's sing one of the old songs we already know. O.K.?"

The question holds merit. One of the overarching benefits of church attendance is that reaffirmation of the most fundamental elements of faith. Among these are: God's supremacy, humankind's fallibility, Jesus' atonement, and the Spirit's indwelling. Comfortable music, like comfort food, satisfies the hungry heart through its rhythms and flowing melodies. It reaches corners of our souls that are difficult to access.

The danger of shutting out new songs lies in our potential to become faith-stagnant to a degree that denies challenge or exposure to fresh thoughts and original expressions. It behooves us to want to know more about God's love so that we might be even more equipped to convey that love to others.

If we draw hard lines that separate us from musical expressions (new to us), if we throw up walls of resistance that blind us from the artistic insights of maturing believers, then what commentary does such a position hold for our faith?

Who says that just because a song is new to us that it is unknown to others? Inquiring minds want to know.

In "choir"ing minds want to know.

*Know us as those who are loved. In the name of the Righteous One we pray.* AMEN.

# 84. Guitars, Combos, and Drums? Oh, My!

*Something tells me we are not in Kansas anymore...unless, of course, you live in Kansas.*

Musical instruments were not intended for Temple use – originally, but acting upon prophetic advice from Gad and Nathan, David gladly incorporated their use, along with choirs, to animate the devotions of the people of Israel.

*Then Hezekiah commanded that the burnt offering be offered on the altar. When the burnt offering began, the song to the Lord began also, and the trumpets, accompanied by the instruments of King David of Israel.*
*~2 Chronicles 29:26*

There is no instrument incapable of giving praise to the Lord. Having said that, we know some instruments detract from worship. Actually, it all depends on where you are and whom you ask. The ones with sanctuaries most certainly do not want drum sets, electric guitars, or tenor saxophones. The ones with worship centers might. The ones with stages most definitely would. More churches than ever before are plugging up and laying down some of the sweetest jazz sounds this side of glory.

Is this a bad thing? No. You see, if all churches were alike, far fewer people would know Jesus as their personal savior. If all church musical expressions were alike, there would be no variety, which gives life and worship its spice. The real question about instrumental appropriateness is the same as it is for any measure of musicality within the consecrated walls of the church. Is the person playing (singing, ringing) to the glory of God, or for personal adulation? The person is either saying, "Hey, look at me," or "Hey, let me point You to God."

Jazz vibes would not work in some congregations any more than red carpet might work with pink walls. Let us assume that all Christian churches are seeking to send the same message. They can do that in multiple ways. The kind of music they use, on average, helps them, perhaps more than any other single thing except for the proclamation of the word, to do that.

If your worship does not sound like a rock concert, you need to worship sometime in a congregation that does. If your worship wails at a high decibel level with pumping speakers and flailing drumsticks, then you need to worship, occasionally, where Godly encounters tend to be more quiet and staid.

*In the name of the Source of our amplification  we pray.*
AMEN.

# XV. Planning Questions

*Church musicians use these questions to lift them above the actions of the moment and require them to think about the matters at hand.*

<u>*Jesus asked Planning Questions:*</u>

- *Which is more important, gold or the Temple? (Matthew)*
- *Can you fast when the Bridegroom is with you? (Mark)*
- *Were ten not cleansed? Where are the nine? (Luke)*
- *Do you believe me now? (John)*

# 85. Do We Need New Hymnals?

*People write music in order to express the ineffable. People put texts to music in order to express the unreachable.*

Praise, out of necessity, should form in the heart before the lips express it.

*Let the word of Christ dwell in you richly; teach and admonish one another in all wisdom; and with gratitude in your hearts, sing psalms, hymns, and spiritual songs to God.*
*~ Colossians 3:16*

The grass is always greener on the other side. When members of your congregation visit other churches, they return to say, *Their hymnal was terrific. It had all the songs we know and love in it. I wish we had that hymnal here.* The fact is, if we got a hymnal together that reflects all of the songs we all know and love, we would have a wonderful, beloved treatise, but there would be one major problem...we would not be able to pick it up!

Congregations shop with confidence when they choose their own denominational hymnals as the chief musical reference for their congregations. After all, such hymnals have been screened for theological content that adheres to the tenets of their faith expression, and they can be purchased with the certainty that each song has been placed under a magnifying glass that the knowledgeable committee has signed off on each page.

Many congregations are free from the pressures exerted on them by denominational thought. As they are free to be the kind of churches they feel led to be, so are they free to select hymnals, or not select hymnals, as they so desire. Technology allows churches the chance to make their own electronic hymnals that place hymns, choruses, and other spiritual songs on large screens. In these places where Christ is magnified, there is no need for book-in-hand singing.

People have definite opinions about their hymnals. Some churches would never go for singing from walls. Others think it silly to be bound to singing old songs that lack contemporary vernacular and innovative chord structures.

Wherever you are, sing with understanding.

*Make our lives go on in endless song. In the name of the Way, the Truth, and the Life we pray,* AMEN.

# 86. Do We Stay in the Choir Loft?

*Nothing makes you feel more like a child of God than when you sing your praise.*

The priests of the Old Testament sacrificed a lamb at the beginning and ending of each day to demonstrate a national sacrifice on behalf of all Israelites.

*Command Aaron and his sons, saying: This is the ritual of the burnt-offering. The burnt-offering itself shall remain on the hearth upon the altar all night until the morning, while the fire on the altar shall be kept burning.*
*~Leviticus 6:9*

After they have sung all of their music for a given service, smaller church choirs usually like to travel from designated choir areas to places where the bulk of their congregations sit. Some choir people love the practice. They get to sit anywhere they want to and with whomever they wish for the remainder of the service. Some choir people hate it. They feel that it is an undignified practice. Further, they figure that they cease to function in their true role as worship leaders the moment they set foot out of their usual location that is set apart for music making.

Staying in the choir loft is viewed as being a more formal practice while moving from the loft is seen as a more relaxed and informal habit. Regardless of where a choir remains during sermon times or during other, longer worship actions, choir people are still choir people. Their significance has not been diminished. Their faith has not shrunk. Their participation in the activities of praise is not past tense.

Larger choirs do not even imagine such. Their sanctuaries, worship centers, or auditoriums are so full of people that it would be difficult to reassemble the choir and/or orchestra in places other than those which have been laid out for them.

Then there are those choirs that are situated in rear balconies on the sides of their consecrated spaces. These choirs are heard and seldom seen anyway. Their migrations from one place to another would be moot if it was done for the purpose of placing them in more comfortable zones.

Choirs need to be mindful that the music is but a portion of the acts of worship that draw us into an awareness of God's presence in our world. Wherever we sit or stand, we are still in that world.

*Seat us by Your Holy side. In the name of the Lamb of God we pray,* AMEN.

# 87.  Does That Have a Soundtrack?

*We can play our favorite, recorded tunes, as many times as we like, knowing that those same tunes will speak to us in a myriad of ways over time.*

Freedom, obtained for the Jews by their Maccbean liberators, did not last for long before they were taken captive by Herodians and Romans.

*When they fall victim, they shall receive a little help, and many shall join them insincerely.*
*~Daniel 11:34*

There is nothing wrong with using an orchestral soundtrack in worship. These are produced beautifully, and they can be depended on, again and again, to render a flawless performance of a song. You get a dimension of sound with an orchestra. You get all of the instrumental colors that make songs come alive in extraordinary ways.

There is nothing wrong with not using an orchestral soundtrack in worship. After all, the person whose finger pushes the play button for the soundtrack has just taken the honor of performance away from those who can play the music "live."

If instrumentalists are available to play for choirs, soloists, and singers, it makes more sense, from a gifts-usage perspective, to encourage them to accompany others. O.K., so that accompaniment runs the risk of not sounding so "Nashville recording studio," but it includes the musical offerings of real people who are real to the life of their congregations.

There are churches out there that would cringe at the thought of using soundtrack accompaniments. There are churches that would be in disbelief that the tracks would not be used or accepted in other places. Never should we negate the motive or the meaning of either brand of church. We are not alike. Praise God, we are not alike.

Regardless of where we are, we need to be on watch for those who can play instruments and work to create opportunities for them to play in worship, even if this practice is not going to be as convenient or polished a custom, as are our pre-recorded orchestras.

*Fill our lives with colorful music. In the name of the Anointed we pray,* AMEN.

# 88. Is the Sound Man Recording This?

[What if you picked up a CD and read these words on it back cover?] *This compact disc is made from analog masters recorded without noise reduction. Half the tracks, in fact, were recorded in a dismal, cheap basement eight-track studio with puddles of water on the floor. Digital technology will now faithfully reproduce these noisy, low-fi, un-professional masters at great expense. Feel stupid yet?*

Writing a letter can be a joyful thing to do. Receiving a letter can be magnificent too. Visiting face to face can be an even greater pleasure.

*Although I have much to write to you, I would rather not use paper and ink; instead I hope to come to you and talk with you face to face, so that our joy may be complete.*
*~2 John 1:12*

Do you remember the first time you ever heard yourself on a playback of a recording? Did you say something like, *I do not sound like that,* or *If I DO sound that way, I am never going to speak again.* Did you? It is that way with audio and video recording the church choir. *Ouch! I'm going on a diet. If others see me the way I just saw myself, whew! I though we sounded pretty good until I listened to that.* You can hear stuff all over the place that needs fixing.

For the performer, music is usually better in the moment. It usually plays better in memory than it does in reproduction. It is almost funny the way we react when we know our sounds and actions are being recorded. We use better posture when sitting or standing. We pay more attention to diction, attacks, releases, dynamic indications and even breath support. It is a tad scary to know that our listeners at church might actually listen –really listen to us, and really watch us to see if our facial and bodily countenances are in concert with our music and its many moods and messages of faith.

Are your services typically recorded? Do you ever listen to your choir from a recording? Why not get into the habit of concentrating in rehearsals in much the same way that you would if you were about to lay your music down on a disc. Try it, and you will be amazed at how much better you sound. Try it, and do the actual recording, and you will be amazed at how much better you sound...that is, until you play it back! Just kidding!

*Wash us, and we will be white as snow. In the name of Jesus we pray,* AMEN.

# 89.  What Are We Doing For Christmas?

*Never B Flat, Never B Sharp, Always B Natural.*

Church music folks look forward to times when special
services of music will waft through their worshipping spaces
to express the totality of emotions that Christ gave to us in
the example of His holy and perfect life.

*He became hungry and wanted something to eat; and while it was*
*being prepared, he fell into a trance.*
*~Acts 10:10*

Sundays come with great regularity. Church musicians are
never more than seven days away from their next scheduled
presentation of musical material. As such, there is a
prevailing concern about readiness that pervades church
musician clusters.

Challenge comes when a musical group is called upon to
lead a church in a musical service that is beyond the call of
typical expectations. The annual Christmas music service
provides an excellent example of the meaning here. When a
singer asks, "What are we doing for Christmas?" there is
two-fold intent: 1.) I am excited about the new music that we
will be learning and 2.) (another question) "Can we learn
this new challenge while simultaneously balancing our
weekly service duties?"

Church choirs hear Sundays calling, *ready or not, here I*
*come.*

This is why the commitment of a choir person is so vital
to the church experience. A person cannot be a part of a
church choir without knowing about extra hours, extra
work, and extra sacrifice. Choir is a commitment that goes
beyond self as it links with others to accomplish mutual
goals. If you desire to do certain things, you must do certain
things to make them become reality.

If you are looking for the easy way, choir is not for you. Choir, praise band, orchestra people never just "go" to church. They are in church, and they are active in church events that prove the adage, *The more you put in to it, the more you get out of it.* Any farmer will tell you that you reap what you sew. And any farmer will tell you that, when all conditions are favorable, you reap more than you sew. So, if that's what we are doing for Christmas, sign me up.

*Collaboration* is the word that best captures this experience of working together to craft worship liturgies."[21]

*Connect us to You. In the name of the Lord of the Sabbath we pray,*
AMEN.

## 90.  Who Will Get the Word Out?

*Music is more than a thing to do. It is a place to be.*

Calvin, the Reformer, said that God could heal the most
desperate sinfulness or backsliding.

*Take words with you and return to the Lord; say to Him 'Take
away all guilt; accept that which is good,' and we will offer the
fruit of our lips.*
*~Hosea 14:2*

Something large is happening here.
Who will get the word out?
Something great and free and clear.
Who will get the word out?

Sounds of heaven's sweet release,
Sounds that angels dare not cease,
Sounds of mercy, love, and peace.
Who will get the word out?

Something big is marching by.
Who will get the word out?
Something filling up the sky.
Who will get the word out?

Beats in rhythms strong pound out,
Beats that make us want to shout.
Beats with zestful worth and clout.
Who will get the word out?

Something huge has called my name.
I will get the word out.
Something higher than all fame.
I will get the word out.

Music spreading wings in flight,
Music lighting up the night,
Music rising as a kite.
I will get the word out!

*In the name of the Root of David we pray,* AMEN.

# XVI. Strategic Questions

*These questions focus on ways to make meaning. These questions arise during data gathering and synthesizing processes.*

*Jesus asked Strategic Questions:*

- *Haven't you ever read what was said to you by God? (Matthew)*
- *What did Moses command you? (Mark)*
- *Why were you searching for me? Did you not know that I must be in my Father's house? (Luke)*
- *My soul is troubled, and what shall I say? (John)*

## 91. Can We Do Something Fun?

*Christians like the companionship of other Christians. Not only is it beneficial for us to worship with like-minded believers, it is crucial that we have fun with them too.*

God brings about salvation, which produces our faith.

*He saved us, not because of any works of righteousness that we had done, but according to his mercy, through the water of rebirth and renewal by the Holy Spirit.*
*~Titus 3:5*

"All we ever do is work on songs that are serious. I wish we could just kick back and have some fun once in a while." Many singers who sign on for church choir echo this sentiment. Music at church has a specific function when it comes to worship, and yet it holds promise in other areas of our lives and for our varied needs as imperfect people.

One of the ways that church music can fill a life need lies in its ability to foster socialization from within the ranks of its participants.[22] When you join a choir at church, you discover that you have become a member of a tiny church within the church. Usually, it is the choir people who have the most fun and do the most things outside of the typical parameters of church membership. Many choir members socialize outside of the walls of the building known as "the church" as they take "the church" to local restaurants, private homes, sporting contests, and cultural events. By so doing, the ministry through music in the church is strengthened by bonds of acquaintance and memory.

Church choir leaders would do well to program something funny, off- the-wall, and out of character from time to time so that choir members can laugh together as they live together. The kinds of experiences suggested here are among the first ones to pop out when church musicians are asked to recount their most favorite church events. Some will even bring out pictures to prove that "so-and-so" once blasted out a song about a turkey, or that "he" was once "she" in an all-male wedding.

Get silly sometimes. Yes, you can do something fun.

*Become the fan that cools our burdens. In the name of Our Shadow From the Heat we pray,* AMEN.

# 92. Did You Know About My Mom's Church...?

*I like all kinds of music except for the kinds that I do not like. How about you?*

We know that when lots were cast for the tribes of Israel, the census of the tribe of Levi was counted by a different rule.

*Inheritance shall be apportioned according to lot between large small.*
*~Numbers 26:56*

That which is done or not done at other people's churches becomes a high-octane topic among church musicians. It is comprehensive and, to be discussed properly, earns the right to be discussed in installments. It is possible that some of these are musical traditions and practices of which you are familiar. Given the diversity of church backgrounds and exposure of the readers of this book though, chances are that most of these will not raise an eyebrow.

- *At my mother's church they have the annual singing Christmas Tree. The singers have to memorize their parts. They are the ornaments on the tree, and ornaments don't hold music.*
- *At the church where I grew up, they don't really have a choir. The song leader selects hymns on the spur of the moment, and asks for volunteers. "Whoever wants to be in the choir today, come on up. It's about time to start the service."*
- *At my cousin's church, they have the local symphony come in one Sunday evening each year to perform a concert. One of the members writes the check for the whole thing.*
- *At my daughter's church, my son-in-law-is the choir director. Their handbell choir rides on a float in the local*

*City Heritage parade, ringing and throwing candy to the children who have come to watch them.*

- *At my neighbor's church the tradition is to make a professionally recorded CD about every other year, featuring the choir's favorite music from that period of time.*
- *At my friend's church, someone got the bright idea to sing through the hymnal in its entirety. So, the choir got together, and for the span of about 24 hours, and in shifts, they sang through their hymnal, cover to cover. The media covered this.*

*Refresh us with the music of others. In the name of the Chosen of God we pray, AMEN.*

# 93.  Did You Perform That In College?

*I do not suppose that we will ever understand exactly what music is or why it does what it does for people who make it and hear it. Like heaven, music is a thing that we reach for but have not yet made contact.*

When Deuteronomy was written, the "latter days" referred to the time when the Messiah would appear, and the scattered tribes if Israel would be reunified and converted to the message of that Messiah.

*Ask now about former ages, long before your own, ever since the day that God created human beings on the earth; ask from one end of heaven to the other: has anything so great as this ever happened or has its like ever been heard of?*
*~Deuteronomy 4:32*

They say the best choir in the world was your college choir.

Upon distributing a warhorse title of music at church, one of those that occupies shelf space in, or at least is known to, many churches across the land, a choir member will declare, "We did this one when I was in college." The intimacy of the moment is surreal. You can see through the singer's distant gaze and knowing smile that the mere mention of the title has provided transport to an earlier time and place when life held so much promise, when dreams had yet to be spun to their real conclusions. The music, the powerful music, is sung again in the singer's memory, where it exists as it did long ago when comrades who were on the threshold of adulthood made it. Like riding a bicycle, once that song was learned it entered the ranks of the never forgotten. Even when the thief of the years dulls the memory to a degree where close friends and even loved ones are hard to call by name, that song and a few special songs like it remain.

Meanwhile, back at the church, the choir has learned the song either for the first time or as re-visited. The funny thing about music is that it never gives you the same experience twice. You, the performer, are not the same, and although the music technically *is* the same, it feels different to you when you sing it again. This is not necessarily a bad thing. Who knows? It might be better in some ways than your college choir.

May God be praised.

*Spin us, as You do Your planets, in perfect orbit. In the name of our Fortress we pray, AMEN.*

# 94. Do We Need a Retreat?

*If you have music in your life, you will have friendship.*

Jesus did not have to train to know how to walk on water.

*When evening came, the boat was out on the lake, and he was alone on the land.*
*~Mark 6:47*

Christian writers have long reminded us of Jesus' pattern of setting Himself apart from His crowds or His entourage when He wanted to pray, fast, and regroup. Church musicians, mindful of that pattern will, at set or random seasons, suggest retreat experiences for themselves and their cohorts. This is normal and natural. Those who minister must also feel that they are ministered unto through the gifts of others. Otherwise, a negative cycle of giving and not receiving takes root, and the ministering one typically crashes and burns or begins to see herself or himself as having superhuman abilities, given the fact that *If it's good for me, then it must be good for God!* Either way, the results are disastrous.

Choir people are usually social people. Think of your church. The choristers are the ones who have the most fun and are the most rowdy. Right? Choir people love the chance to take retreats together. Numerous choirs will take retreats in order to jump start music learning for special projects that are hard to tackle along with preparing music for ongoing, customary worship.

Choir people are sacred people. Their measures of dedication to the Lord through the church are evident and real. Retreats afford them the chance to recharge their batteries. It is a good thing. Choir spouses usually come along for the ride. Neighbors who seldom see each other long enough to chat are given an excuse through the retreat experience to do just that. It helps them to move beyond the *How are you? I am fine. You?* stage and on to something more meaningful and satisfying.

Those who know and like one another...these are the ones who stand the chance of making heavenly music.

*Center us in Your ways. In the name of Emmanuel, God With Us, we pray,* AMEN.

# 95. May I Take Some Time Off?

*Some go to church for a message in song. They usually find at least one, but not always where they look or suspect.*

We plant seeds. We expect the seeds to grow into what they are. The seeds must be watered and exposed to the sun.

*Let what you heard from the beginning abide in you. If what you heard from the beginning abides in you, then you will abide in the Son and in the Father.*
*~1 John 2:24*

My days are hard, and I am spent.
At times I wonder where time went.
The choir is something that can go.
I bet that I will miss it, though.

The kids, the spouse, they all need me
To escort them from A to Z.
No time for song, I think I'll scream.
No time for fun or peach ice cream.

Just work, that's all. "You're nice to phone.
The choir won't miss my baritone.
I'll come right back when things are still.
But now they rage against my will."

"You don't believe that I'll come back
To place my hymnal in the rack?
O.K., well, fine. That's some retort!
You're not, I think, a real good sport."

"Instead of cutting me some slack;
You'll prob'ly talk behind my back,
And say that my commitment lags

Behind each time my vigor sags."

"Goodbye, my choir director, friend."
Now to my issues I will tend.

*Return us to our calling. In the name of the Lord of the Living and the Dead we pray, AMEN.*

# 96. Where Are All of Our People?

*Music bears fruit. There is nothing Christians can experience that*
*music cannot reflect to some degree.*

If you think about it, all of us are doing some-thing at all
times. In following that thought, all of us are similarly somewhere at all times. Let us develop the habit of frequently
asking ourselves where we are and what we are doing.

*Therefore, thus says the LORD, the God of Israel, concerning the*
*shepherds who shepherd my people: It is you who have scattered*
*my flock, and have driven them away, and you have not attended*
*to them. So I will attend to you for your evil doings, says the*
*LORD.*
*~Jeremiah 23:2*

- It is raining cats and dogs. The Baptists are happy,
  because the chance of total immersion has increased.
- It is a holiday weekend. The Catholics are pleased, for
  they have more feasts to celebrate than any other
  group of believers.
- Kids don't have school tomorrow. That means the
  Methodists will go out of town.
- Since we are having that big thing tonight, he is not
  coming this morning. Lutherans!
- They have out of town house guests. No one
  entertains quite like the Presbyterians.
- He is very sick. Flu, I think I heard someone say. Do
  non/inter denominationalists get more colds?

Where are all of our people?

- The evening pot-luck supper has been cancelled.
  Don't look for the Church of God brothers and sisters
  to be there.

- The back pews of the church have been removed. Where will the Pentecostals sit?
- The Episcopalians are boycotting. Someone dared to say that prayer is not "common."
- The African Methodist Episcopalians are hurt that someone confused them with the Christian Methodist Episcopalians.
- Summer is here. That means that the Disciples of Christ are not.
- The Quakers are upset to the point of being un"friend"ly.

Where are all our people?
Where should they be?

*I was glad when they said unto me, 'Let us go into the house of the Lord.'*

*Follow us when we stray. In the name of the Prince of Life we pray,* AMEN.

pastors and peoples together as one voice, singing the same song, and marching in the same metric form.

When it works it is a beautiful thing, a beautiful thing indeed.

*Shepherd us, O God. In the name of the Son of the Highest we pray,* AMEN.

# 98. Do You Need a "Gold Star"?

*Some say that all songs are out there somewhere waiting to be discovered by composers. Those same people feel that sculptors merely find what already lives and lays hidden in their stones.*

We think that certain things are just ours- only for us. Just because you spend a lot of time around something does not mean that it belongs to you.

*Then pay attention to how you listen; for to those who have, more will be given; and from those who do not have, even what they seem to have will be taken away.*
*~Luke 8:18*

Are you in a choir where the director plays favorites? Why is it that there are those chosen few who get all of the attention, glory, and slack, when everyone else is treated like union labor by an unconcerned management? In football, we often see special decals adhered to the helmets of players who have distinguished themselves by making outstanding plays. The players themselves, or maybe their key position coaches, based on careful review of game films, perhaps, vote on these. Or maybe, just maybe they are handed out, pell-mell, by the selective head coach, to those favorite tenors, that too-good for words altos, that tiny handful of sopranos, or that he-thinks-he's all that and a bag of chips bass.

The game of favorites is probably not being played. It is all in your imagination. If, however, the game of favorites is being played, maybe there is a reason. Maybe the director knows the person is ultra committed to the ministry of music through the church. Maybe the person has the kind of personality that responds well to constant affirmation. Maybe the person is so talented that the director does not want to lose him or her to Sister Church Down the Street through a sin of neglect.

Why does it bother you anyway? Could it be that you would like to be more committed but are not? Is it possible that you are above the need to be wheedled? Is it possible – dare the word be used –that you are a teeny bit *jealous* of their gifts?

Do not ask your directors, for your directors were once those favorite people of their former directors. Your directors would be very confused by your question.

*Love us, for we are special in Your sight. In the name of our Passover we pray,* AMEN.

# 99.  Did You Hear That On Television?

*I do not like certain kinds of music, but I do not wish to disparage those who do. And, for those of you who like the kinds of music that I do not, disparage means "make fun of."*

Make what you do *from the Lord.*

*Hold to the standard of sound teaching that you have heard from me, in the faith and love that are in Christ Jesus.*
*~2 Timothy 1:18*

One of the challenges that choir people must face is the temptation of comparison. When readying for church attendance, there are those who watch televised church services before their cars roll out of their driveways and head in the direction of their own churches. They will be impressed by the sheer magnitude of every shot conveyed by the camera.[23] The choir will be bigger and better than theirs is. The pastor will be more handsome (or beautiful) than theirs. The sermon will be more relevant to daily life. The choir director will not be as bald as is theirs. The orchestra will be fantastic. That televised church will seem to have it all and have all that they have together, presented incomparably. Simply magnificent!

Then, they drive to their own churches. Reality sets in. Their choir is not as great in number, and it does not knock you over with sound power or rare beauty. The pastor does not look like a movie star. The sermon will sound a lot like a sermon that was preached six months ago. The choir director's head will be the most prominent shining star in the building. The orchestra? There is no orchestra. Are you kidding? Worship does not seem to flow as smoothly as it did on television. There are no close ups, no pans, just real people worshiping live, in real time.

They will say to the director, "Why can't we do music like the Church of the Redeemed in Indianapolis. You know the one that comes on Channel 32 on Sunday mornings? That church is growing, and it has to be because of that fantastic music."

"That church has 150 choir members each time they sing in their services," the director will say, "And we only have 15."

"Well, if we did their music, we would be as large in number as they are," the well-intentioned singer will say.

O green-eyed monster, get behind us, and don't push.

*Forgive our needless comparisons. In the name of the Rabbi we pray, AMEN.*

# 100. When Did We Last Clean Our Robes?

*Every once in a while, shut out all of life and completely immerse yourself in music. Let it roll over you. Roll with it.*

Jesus talked about cleanliness in its various forms.

*Jesus said to him, 'One who has bathed does not need to wash, except for the feet, but is entirely clean. And you are clean, though not all of you.'*
*~John 13:10*

"Whose robe is this?" the new choir member whose robe had yet to be assigned, asked as the choir was preparing for morning worship. "Let's see," the seasoned veteran soprano said with an air of confidence. "Oh, it's Bea's robe. Ask me how I know that. (Not waiting for a response) Because I smell her cologne all over it. Don't take that one. It's Bea's."

Choir robes can get lost in the weekly shuffle of things. After all, choirs only wear them for short periods of time and usually on only one day of the week. The dry cleaning of choir robes is not the most important item for a church to be anxious over, yet it is symbolic of something very, very important.

Within Christian circles there is much talk about people's sins being washed "whiter than snow." When we clean our choir robes, we are not saying that the scent of Bea's cologne is so oppressive that it needs to be removed. We are saying that, from time to time, we need to take an inventory of our lives. We need spiritual tune-ups, check-ups, spring cleanings, tidying ups. Those robes look the same, for the most part, after they are cleaned, but the wearers of them feel as refreshed and invigorated as if they themselves have been put through the same organic solvents as have the robes.

Soon, Bea's cologne will again find its lingering way into the warp and woof of the garment known as the "choir robe." Thank God, for that means that Bea is using it for an instrument of devotion. When we work, things get dirty. Praise God!

*Wash us. In the name of the Nazarene we pray,* AMEN.

# 101. Who Is Running the Sound Board?

*Be brand new.*

In Christ we become new creations, putting away the old and holding steadfast to the new, much in the same way as a butterfly comes forward from its chrysalis.

*...The only thing that counts is faith expressing itself through love.*
~Galatians 5: 6

The poor, poor sound person of the church. This person is an unsung hero. The sound woman or man spends time before, during, and after services to ensure that all of the choreography of worship is captured so that all can see and hear. This is not an easy assignment.

The sound person sets up microphone chords and stands, works with recording devices, lights, controls, mixing boards and wireless microphones...the list could go on, and the work proceeds with great anonymity until feedback is heard or until a single note is not carried to the back of the house by a soloist. Then, it happens. People begin to turn around. They turn around to see if there is any person sitting at the controls. Most everyone turns around, even the person who has had neck problems for years and cannot turn his neck, turns around. They give a stare as if to say, "Are you going to fix that?" It is a terrible look that sends chills down the spine of every Christian sound/light technician. The moments feel like hours. The problem is corrected. They resume their natural seated positions. After the service, someone will come up to the sound person and tell her or him that there was a "problem with the sound today."

It takes a special person to be a technical operations person within the life of a worshiping church. In some instances, a sound person will actually practice with the musicians. This, when it is possible, is an excellent way to head off issues before they arise. Practicing together ends most of the pre-service scrambling, and it brings the technical folks on board as part of the team that leads in worship. Find your sound people. Thank them for their ministry among the people.

*In the name of the King of Kings we pray,* AMEN.

# 102. Procession? Recession?

*Some jokingly call the processional the "in-trot."*

The praise of God has a place, a mode, and a theme. May it be said of us that we did our duty with gusto.

*For everything there is a season, and a time for every matter under heaven.*
*~Ecclesiastes 3:1*

The hardest thing for choirs will never reside within the music itself. The hardest thing for choirs is moving from Point A to Point B. It is the tradition of many choirs to process and/or recess at times of worship. When new members join in, the movement of it all immediately challenges them. "Who is on my left, and who is on my right?" they will ask as they wait in the Narthex to enter the service. It all seems a bit strange. "Remember, we have to save a seat for Marge on the front row. She will be here, but she is not here right now." The new member marvels at the precision with which things maneuver for the choir's entrance into worship.

When recessing, the effort does not lose its tension, because the times when choirs exit their worship spaces, they typically do so in a manner that is exactly opposite to that in which they gained their entry. Therefore, maybe you had a grip on the access. Now you have to understand the egress.

Worship, in most any configuration, contains elements of choreography, a term that suggests dance in at one level or another. True to its name, *worship* means "the work of the people." That work involves people standing, sitting, kneeling, walking, and so forth. Kierkegaard's famous statement about worship, often quoted, is a vivid representation of what is going on in most any church, or what should be, at any given time in worship:

> In the most earnest sense, God is the critical theatergoer, who looks on to see how the lines are spoken and how they are listened to. Hence, here the customary audience is wanting. The speaker is then the prompter, and the listener stands openly before God. The listener...is the actor, who in all truth acts before God.[24]

So, if you play in the handbell choir, sing in the church choir, or direct a children's choir, come to church with your running shoes. You just might find yourself doing a bit of traveling.

*Go with us as we take Your message from place to place,    O God*, AMEN.

# Post Scriptum

All of the people with whom I have made music have contributed to the creation of this book. I am thinking of key people who have added to my development as a person and as a professional. If you are holding this book, and if your life has intersected mine at church at some point during our shared journey of life, then you have contributed to this creation. Thank you.

Especially I appreciate the following people for inspiring much of the material for this book. Their friendship and dedication to church music helped this manuscript to shape into its completed form–

...The Rev. Monty Nelson, for being my pastor and encourager.

...Anna Blackledge, Jeff Blair, Karen Bouchard, Paul Christensen, Kay Coots, Peggy Deurelle, Aimee Fletcher, Clay Hobbs, Nancy Owens, Bebelynn Rodriguez, and Mary Smisson, for choral insights.

...Bobby Sisk, for the "guru" factor.

...Penny Nelson and Renee Powers, for conferences about keyboards.

...Jackie Bishoff, Ross Bishoff, Amelia Blair, Charlotte Blair, Karen Fletcher, Zak Fletcher, Heather Hobbs, and Elaine Roller, for handbell matters.

...Amy Line, for instrumental consultations.

...Miriam Moncrief, for holding down the fort.

...Jeff Killip and Randy Pinson, for having "sound" ideas.

...Robbin Roling and Irma Johnson, for telling children about Jesus.

...Claudia Markov, for her talents of organization.

...and, of course, Martha Powell, for earning the most "gold stars."

Ahem... I can hear all of you and others too.

# End Notes

*References to Scripture come from the New Revised Standard Version of the Holy Bible.*

## Introduction

[1]Stock, G. (1987). *The Book of Questions*. New York: Workman Publishing Company.

[2]Browne, N. & Keeley, S. (2000). *Asking the Right Questions* (6th Ed.). Upper Saddle River, NJ: Prentice Hall.

[3]Miller, J. (2004). *QBQ! The Question Behind the Question*. New York: G. P. Putnam's Sons.

[4]Merton, T. (1970). *Opening the Bible*. Louisville, KY: The Merton Legacy Trust.

[5]McKenzie, J. (1997). Creating research programs for an age of information. *From Now On: A Technology Journal*, (7)2, October.

## I

[6]Dodd, P. & Sundheim, D. (2005). *25 Best Time Management Tools & Techniques: How to Get More Done Without Driving Yourself Crazy*. Chelsea, MI: Peak Performance Press, Inc.

## II

[7]Lorayne, H. & Lucas, J. (2000). *The Memory Book: The Classic Guide to Improving Your Memory at Work, at School, and at Play*. New York: Ballantine Books:

# III

[8]Lloyd, M. (2009). *Supercharged Retirement: Ditch the Rocking Chair, Trash the Remote, and Do What You Love.* University Place, WA: Hankfritz Press.

[9]Frankl, V. (2006). *Man's Search for Meaning.* Boston: Beacon Press.

# IV

[10]Fortang, L. (2005). *Now What? 90 Days to a New Life Direction.* New York: Tarcher/Penguin.

# V

[11]Donoghue, P. & Siegel, M. (2005). *Are You Really Listening? Keys to Successful Communication.* Notre Dame, IN: Sorin Books.

# VI

[12]Maxwell, J. (2007). *The 21 Irrefutable Laws of Leadership: Follow Them and People Will Follow You.* Nashville, TN: Thomas Nelson.

# VII

[13]Sandholtz, K., Derr, B., Carlson, D., & Buckner, K. (2002). *Beyond Juggling: Rebalancing Your Busy Life.* San Francisco, CA: Berrett-Koehler Publishers.

## VIII

[14]Conner, M. (2004). *Learn More Now: 10 Simple Steps to Learning Better, Smarter, and Faster*. Hoboken, NJ: Wiley.

## IX

[15]Maas, J. (1998). *Power Sleep: The Revolutionary Program That Prepares Your Mind for Peak Performance*. New York: Collins Living.

## X

[16]Gill, L. (1999). *How to Work With Just About Anyone: A 3-Step Solution for Getting Difficult People to Change*. New York: Fireside.

## XI

[17]Sanford, J. (1982). *Ministry Burnout*. Louisville, KY: Westminster John Knox Press

## XII

[18]Carter, L. (2007). *When Pleasing You Is Killing Me*. Nashville, TN: B&H Publishing Group.

## XIII

[19]Felder, L. (2008). *Fitting In Is Overrated: The Survival Guide for Anyone Who Has Ever Felt Like an Outsider*. New York: Sterling Publishing.

# XIV

[20]Jewell, J. (2004). *Wired for Ministry: How the Internet, Visual Media, and Other New Technologies Can Serve Your Church.* Ada, MI: Brazos Press.

# XV

[21]Vanderwell, H., & de Waal Malefyt, N. (2005). *Designing Worship Together: Models and Strategies For Worship Planning (Vital Worship, Healthy Congregations).* Herndon, VA: The Alban Institute.

# XVI

[22]Mancini, W. (2008). *Church Unique: How Missional Leaders Cast Vision, Capture Culture, and Create Movement.* San Francisco, CA: Jossey-Bass.

# XVII

[23]MacDonald, G. (2008). *Who Stole My Church?: What to Do When the Church You Love Tries to Enter the 21st Century.* Nashville, TN: Thomas Nelson.

[24]Oden, T. (Ed.). (1978). *Parables of Kierkegaard,* Princeton, NJ: Princeton University Press.

# Topical Index

*(number refers to order, not page)*